PRINCESS ASCENDING

A Royal Progress in Two Acts
by
Norman Holland

A Salute to Her Majesty Queen Elizabeth II
On the Occasion of Her Silver Jubilee
1952 – 1977

SAMUEL FRENCH

LONDON
NEW YORK   TORONTO   SYDNEY   HOLLYWOOD

PHOTO-LITHO REPRINT BY W & J MACKAY LIMITED, CHATHAM
FROM EARLIER IMPRESSION

PRINCESS ASCENDING

For Peggy Batchelor, gifted actress, talented teacher,
woman of the theatre

PRINCESS ASCENDING

The play was first produced at the Club Theatre, Altrincham, on 23rd January, 1977, with the following cast:

Emma		Valerie Harris
Rose	Ladies-in-Waiting to	Pat Kirkman
Margaret	Princess Elizabeth	Cherrill Wyche
Nell		Pauline Jackson
Lady Jane Grey		Debbie Highland
Queen Mary		Irene Burgess
Kate Ashley		Freda Studley
Princess Elizabeth		Pat Lawrence
Zuleika Daniels		Mona Brundrett
Jane The Fool		Avis Lux
Lady Alicia Mordaunt	Ladies-in-Waiting to	Jacqueline Powell
Lady Harriet Scrope	Queen Mary	Kathleen Dunworth
The Commons of England		The Audience

Directed by
Vicki Lane

The action of the play takes place in Queen Mary's Palaces, the various residences where Princess Elizabeth was detained, and the Tower of London. The scene remains unchanged throughout.

Time—1553–1558

Words of the anthem/lullaby by Norman Holland
Music by Ian Pearson
Cover design by Virginia Coan

AUTHOR'S NOTE

Although I have, on several occasions, used the actual words spoken by Lady Jane Grey, Queen Mary and Princess Elizabeth, I have not been entirely faithful to historical fact in that I have transposed events and invented others. Zuleika is an invented character but Jane the Fool did exist and Queen Mary, ever careful with money, grudged the fourpence (one groat!) it cost her every time Jane's head was shaved.

The song "Back and side, go bare, go bare", is a very old English drinking song and it predates the Elizabethan era by at least a century or two. It can be sung to the tune of "The Lincolnshire Poacher". Music is provided for the lullaby/anthem, the words of which are mine, but I do not accept responsibility for the couplet which is quoted as having been worked over the cradle in Mary's nursery. This is copied verbatim from contemporary sources.

A record-player will be needed to produce some of the effects and Samuel French can provide a recording of a peal of bells though a knell can be produced by striking a bell with a hammer at regularly spaced intervals but, if this does not seem practical, Samuel French can provide a recording of a Funeral Bell.

There is, in the dialogue, a buried Shakespearean quotation, but no prize is offered for identifying it.

N.H.

ACT I

The setting is curtained and preferably dark so that the costumes can be seen to advantage against the background. There are entrances L and R

Up c there is a throne-like chair set on a dais. Over the chair is a canopy upon which appears the device of a golden crown. There are two stools—R and L of the chair

Trumpets sound a fanfare. Four young women (Emma, Rose, Margaret and Nell) enter—two by way of each entrance. They are dressed in fashion of the English Court of 1553. Facing the audience, they form a line and wait until the fanfare ends. Then they curtsy in unison

All May it please your Graces and you, the Commons of England, we are four well-born maids.

Emma (*curtsying*) Emma . . .

Rose (*curtsying*) Rose . . .

Margaret (*curtsying*) Margaret . . .

Nell (*curtsying*) And Nell.

All Four well-born maids who serve Elizabeth, a great princess . . .

Nell Who today, by reason of her birth, stands in some peril.

Margaret Consider this troubled realm of England . . .

Rose In this year of grace fifteen hundred and fifty-three.

Emma Seven years ago, great Henry, eighth English King of that name, died . . .

Nell And his only son, a saintly boy, reigned . . .

Margaret With the help of a Lord Protector and a Council

Rose Now is Edward, sixth English King of that name,

Emma Most untimely dead.

All four place their fingertips together, bow their heads and briefly mourn Edward. Nell is the first to disengage her fingers and raise her head

Nell You must understand that King Henry had two—(*she raises two fingers*)—outstanding talents.

Margaret One was for music . . .

The music of "Greensleeves" is heard. As if entranced, all listen with hands clasped and heads to one side in exactly the same attitude. Again, it is Nell who breaks the spell. She makes a quelling gesture in the direction of the music and it ceases abruptly

Nell This music does not help us. Where had we reached in this, our chronicle?

Rose I was about to disclose King Henry's other outstanding talent.

Emma Then do so, girl. Do so.

Rose (*confidentially*) King Henry's other outstanding talent was for——

Rose draws a deep breath and the others join in when she says

All —marrying.

Rose Which he did on six separate occasions.

All (*nodding*) Six separate occasions.

They each raise their hands and hold up six fingers. Then they lower their hands, shake their heads and make clicking noises expressive of disapproval. Emma's raised hand is the signal for silence. She then gives them the beat and they sing as if rendering a psalm

(*Singing*) In all great Henry did espouse
          A couple of Annes,
          No fewer than three Catherines
          And a single Jane.

Emma Who, by birth, stands nearest to the dead young King?

Rose There is Lady Jane Grey, grand-daughter of great Henry's sister.

Margaret There is our shining Princess Elizabeth, daughter of King Henry and Anne Boleyn.

Nell And Mary, daughter of Henry by Catherine, his first wife.

All But it is Mary, Mary, who shall reign.

There is a flourish of trumpets

Emma But, in despite of her, ruthless ambitious men have proclaimed Lady Jane Grey as Queen.

Rose But these men are overthrown.

Margaret Overthrown, captured, imprisoned or executed.

All But not Lady Jane Grey. Sweet and scholarly, mild and obedient, she awaits judgement.

Then, shouting

          Stand aside! Make way! Make way!
          For the Lady Jane Grey!
          Let us hear what she has to say!

They move in disciplined unison and stand so that they surround an inner area

Lady Jane Grey, a soberly dressed girl of sixteen, comes in carrying a book, and stands in the midst of them. She looks from face to face and is intimidated by their stern expressions. She falters

Jane Give you good morrow, good ladies.

Emma Is it good morrow?

Rose For us it may be.

Margaret Not for you. Not for you.

Nell Are you not the Lady Jane Grey?

Puzzled, Jane looks from one to the other

Jane But you know me and all of you are known to me. I could name each one of you. (*Pointing to Nell*) You are the Lady——

Emma (*interrupting*) That is not the question.

Rose What is your lineage?

Margaret Who are you, Lady Jane Grey?

Jane I should not need to tell you.

All But you must. Tell us your degree.
  Pronounce in full your pedigree.

Jane Then hearken: I am the grand-daughter of Mary Tudor, sister of King Henry the Eighth, and I am the daughter of John Grey, Duke of Suffolk, Marquess of Dorset, and of Frances, his wife, daughter of the aforesaid Mary Tudor.

Emma And is that all?

Jane All? You wish for more?

Rose Surely, mistress, you are altogether over-modest?

Margaret Are you not the most exalted lady in this realm?

Nell Were you not styled Jane the First?

Emma Were you not so proclaimed?

All (*pointing to her*) Answer! Answer now!

Jane I was indeed so proclaimed—by my father. It was not by my wish. I had no part in the proclamation but did as I was bid as an obedient daughter. My father was in error.

Emma That much is true.

Jane The poor man is to pay with his life.

Rose So perish all traitors to the true Queen Mary!

Jane Now that I have told you who I am, now that I have told you that I was proclaimed Queen against my will, may I go home? Oh, may I now go home?

The four Ladies-in-Waiting join hands and circle Jane, chanting as they do so, as if rendering a nursery-rhyme

All All in vain! All in vain!

Emma The Duke of Suffolk did proclaim

Rose His young daughter as Queen Jane.

All Hey down! All in vain! All in vain!

Margaret The Duke of Suffolk will lose his head.

Nell The Duke of Suffolk will lie dead.

All Hey down! All in vain! All in vain!

Emma And the Queen he did proclaim

Rose Is but a poor lost girl again.

All Hey down! All in vain! All in vain!

With the last words, they loose hands and curtsy deeply. As they rise, Jane addresses them

Jane Sweet Ladies, you do not answer me. May I go home? I am not one for crowns and courts, not for princes and palaces. I am but a poor, quiet girl who loves my study and my garden, my books and flowers and yes, my dog, Patch, who will be missing me this long time past.

Emma Where is your father, the great Duke of Suffolk?

Jane Why, he is in prison, as all men do know.

Emma And he awaits a traitor's death. That, too, all men do know.

Rose And where is your husband, Lord Guildford Dudley?

Jane He is—he is . . . (*She falters*)

Rose (*implacably*) Come, girl, where is he?

Jane (*weeping*) He is dead. You all know that he is dead. I saw—I saw his body in the cart.

Margaret Then you are answered. There is no going home for you. You are one with the rest.

Nell Nay, you are more. You are a rallying-point for traitors.

Emma As such you have been condemned.

All You must die.

Jane Why then, I must. But as I go to meet my God, you must believe the words I spoke when they named me as heir to the Crown of England. My words were these: "The Crown is not my right and pleaseth me not. The Lady Mary is the rightful heir."

Emma But your action belied those words.

Rose And it is for that you are to die.

Jane gives her prayer-book to Emma

Jane Good friend, take this, my prayer book. See that it is conveyed to my father. Haply, it will comfort him. Tell him that I died a Christian girl in the sure and certain expectation of everlasting life. Tell him that I forgive him as I hope to be forgiven and I believe that I shall see him hereafter in a glorious morning. Where—where is it to be done?

Rose (*bringing forward one of the stools and setting it down*) Here. You must kneel here.

Jane goes and stands behind the stool. She looks sad and pensive

Jane I wish . . .

Emma What is your wish?

Jane You cannot help me. It is just that I truly hope somebody will be kind to poor Patch. He is a very foolish dog but he loves me well. (*She peers fearfully beyond them*) Is this—is this the man who will . . .?

Emma This is the headsman—the executioner.

Jane (*looking off into the shadows*) Then I forgive you, friend. You are but the instrument of the Queen's justice. I thank God of His great goodness that he has given me a time and respite to repent. (*Then she turns and addresses the audience directly*) And now, good people, while I am alive, I pray you assist me with your prayers. (*Again, she turns and looks into the shadows*) Now I shall kneel and let it be done when I stretch forth my hands—so. (*She illustrates. Then she kneels behind the stool*) Have mercy upon me, oh God!

Jane leans forward, places her head upon the stool and stretches out her hands as she had done a moment before. As she does so, there is an immediate Black-out and, in the darkness, there is heard the crash of the axe striking the block. Briefly, the darkness prevails and then light grows slowly from a promise to fulfilment. The stool has been restored to its place near the chair. The four girls are standing motionless in attitudes of mourning

Emma Now has she passed from Time into Eternity.

Rose Now is the world the poorer for the loss of a true, sweet maid.
Margaret Now her flowers bloom without her and her books gather dust.
Nell Now Patch, her dog, looks for her in vain.
Emma And who is she who consented to the death of poor Jane?
Rose Yes, who approved?
Margaret Who acquiesced?
Nell Who assented?
Emma Mary Tudor, Queen of England!

Mary enters R, crowned and erect. She is thirty-seven years of age, soberly but richly dressed and she is dark and of medium size. After a brief pause, she walks slowly back and forth as if in contemplation. She avoids contact with the group

Emma Lonely and uncertain, she moves with a show of arrogance among her subjects.
Rose She is wholly possessed by one overmastering resolve which is . . .
Margaret To restore this realm to the Catholic faith.
Nell And to root out, punish and destroy all those she considers to be unbelievers.

Mary pauses at the farthest remove from the four girls

Emma Hers is truly the power of life and death. For she summons——

Mary beckons imperiously. Emma stands unmoving and observing. The other three girls move forward in line towards the Queen who points to a spot indicating where they are to stand and face her. They pause in unison and curtsy deeply. They stand patiently before her until she continues

—and she dismisses.

Mary makes a disdainful gesture of dismissal. The three curtsy again and, still in line, move backwards respectfully. They halt at some distance from Mary and Emma joins them. All four regard the Queen apprehensively

Emma This Queen does not care for the scent of flowers.
Rose Nor does she take pleasure in the provocation of perfume.
Margaret Her taste is otherwise.
Nell Far otherwise.
Mary Open now the windows! Fling wide the doors! I would fill my nostrils with that which most pleases me in all the world—the stench of burning heretics! (*She raises her head, breathes deeply and her expression reflects the burning religious fanaticism within. Momentarily sated, she smiles unpleasantly*) We are well pleased! We are indeed very well pleased! For once the wind blows from the right quarter! (*She becomes once more aware of the presence of the girls*) They burn in agony as they will burn hereafter to expiate their sinful unbelief. For what good it will do, pray now for the repose of their souls. And now I take my leave of you.

Mary pauses only to acknowledge the girls' deep curtsies with a dismissive nod; then she goes out as she entered, R

The girls gaze after her fearfully. When they have assured themselves that she is out of earshot, they face the front again .

Emma Now you have seen her.
Rose Now you have seen the Queen of England.
Margaret What is your view of her? Is she not royal?
Nell Oh, she is royal enough.
Emma If she is all you have seen of royalty.
Rose Queen Mary burns heretics that she may win favour with the Pope.
Margaret With the Pope and with the King of Spain
Nell Whose son she hopes to marry
Emma For the furtherance of the Catholic cause.
Rose Oh, Queen Mary is passing royal in her fashion.
Margaret But not so royal as our Princess.
Nell When the Queen rode in triumph into London
Emma Our Princess rode at her side.
Rose The Queen shone.
Emma Our Princess blazed.
Margaret The Queen was a lanthorn.
Emma Our Princess was the sun.
Nell For the Princess Elizabeth is a paragon of perfection.
Emma A miracle of grace,
Rose A masterpiece of majesty
Margaret And she is more royal than the Queen . . .
Nell Infinitely more royal.
Emma (*looking off* R) But you shall judge for yourselves for here she comes . . .
Rose The great and gracious Princess Elizabeth,
Margaret True heir to the Crown of England!

But it is not the Princess Elizabeth who enters from the R but Kate Ashley, a soberly dressed woman of fifty who pauses in annoyance when all four girls greet her with a shout of laughter

Kate What ails you idle wenches that you make mock of your betters?
Margaret Nay, Kate, good, sweet Kate, do not chide.
Nell We had thought to see the Princess and you came timely in.

Emma detaches herself from the group and comes down to address the audience

This, as you see, is not the Princess Elizabeth but Kate Ashley, her friend and confidante, her some-time governess and her trusted familiar.
Kate And what do you here? Is this not the hour of day when you should be at your embroidery frames?
Emma (*rejoining the group*) Dear Kate, sweet Kate, we are out of silks.
Rose We are out of red silk, blue silk and yellow.
Margaret But we are well furnished with grey, brown and purple.
Nell All colours which we do not need.

All four Ladies-in-Waiting are facing towards Kate which means that they do not see Elizabeth enter

Elizabeth enters L. She is twenty years of age and reflects something of the appearance and qualities credited to her by her ladies. If possible, she should wear a costume lighter in colour than those worn by the rest of the characters. Particularly when she was young, she favoured brightly coloured clothes. Here the intention is to direct attention to her—to set her apart from the rest

Emma Procure some silks for us, dear Kate.
All (*crowding round Kate*) Do so! Do so! Do so, good Kate!

Kate sees Elizabeth and makes a quelling gesture which silences the girls

Kate Peace . . .

There is that in her glance which causes the girls to turn and face Elizabeth

Good morrow to your Grace.

All curtsy deeply as the other ladies repeat:

All Good morrow to your Grace.
Elizabeth Give you good morrow, ladies. Pray that we see better days than this.
Kate What news, my lady? You were busy with messengers, Councillors, Ministers of State . . .
Elizabeth Nay, Kate, not I. They were busy with me—and not to my benefit. I am summoned.
Kate Summoned, my lady?
Elizabeth To the Queen's Palace at Whitehall.
Kate To what end?
Elizabeth To be examined as to my involvement in the late rebellion. To be questioned as to my connections with the traitors and conspirators— living and dead.
Kate But good, my lady, all the world knows that you had no part in the rebellion, no correspondence with the rebels.
Elizabeth Not all the world, Kate. There were those among the Commissioners just now who eyed me doubtfully and who heard my protestations with an air of mocking unbelief.
Emma But, most gracious lady, suspicions count for nothing. There exists no proof that you had any part in the late rebellion.
Elizabeth Then, whether it exists or not, these Commissioners will find it.

Elizabeth goes over to the dais and seats herself on the chair. The others follow and form a sympathetic group in the near neighbourhood of the chair

These are dedicated men who are sworn to seek out, arrest, bring to trial and put to death all those who had a hand in the uprising. God knows I am none of these. I know myself to be wholly innocent but I do confess to you—I do confess . . .
Margaret Yes, my lady?
Elizabeth To a mounting feeling of guilt when, as just now, I met the unrelenting stare of the Commissioners. I was other than myself. I

guarded my tongue—hesitated before I spoke—watched my words. As for them, they observe—take note—draw conclusions. They are still here—still in the hall below.

Margaret But they will not stay here. Take heart, gracious lady. Soon they will be gone.

Elizabeth Go or stay—all's one to me. I am soon to meet with them again at Whitehall. You know what my fear is, Kate?

Kate What, my lady?

Elizabeth That there will be some poor, tortured prisoner who, to save himself from the continued agony of the rack, will shriek the syllables of my name. That will be enough. It will give them all the proof they need.

Rose Can you not appeal for clemency to the Queen?

Elizabeth That I can—but to do so would be to argue that I am guilty. (*She rises*) Even so, I hope to put my case to Her Majesty. But these are my griefs—not yours. You were best to part from me here and now. I am allowed to take with me the people of my household but I shall not take it amiss if any or all of you decide not to bear me company.

Kate I shall be of your troop, Princess.

Emma And I.

Rose I, too.

Margaret I have, your Grace, a great liking for the Palace of Whitehall.

Kate As for me, I have never been within the Palace. Herein is my opportunity.

Elizabeth Bless you, dear Kate. Thanks and thanks again, good wenches. (*She is down among them, impulsively, pressing their hands. Then she draws away from them*) But it were best that you know what you hazard. We have been kept close here at Ashridge. But this, they claimed, was for our protection. They were guarding the heir to the Throne. We shall be close confined in Whitehall and closer yet if—if . . .

Kate If?

Elizabeth If I am sent to the Tower. You would do well to think upon it.

There is a brief silence. Then Emma bursts out

Emma Your royal Highness, they would not dare!

Elizabeth Would not dare?

Emma To imprison a princess of Tudor blood in the Tower.

Elizabeth Would not dare! They would dare more than that! Much, much more. Tell me this: where is that high-born maid of Tudor blood, Lady Jane Grey?

The ladies exchange uneasy glances

I will not press you for an answer but will tell you where she is. She is the shorter by a head and she lies in a shallow grave within the confines of the Tower. There is great danger in my service. I say again—think upon the hazard. Think well upon it! I shall not think the less of any one of you if she decides not to come with me.

Elizabeth nods with an air of finality and sweeps out L

All curtsy as she departs. There is the briefest, uncertain pause

Emma I follow the Princess.

Emma exits L

Rose And I.
Nell And I.

Rose and Nell exit L

Margaret stands stock-still, gazing after her departed friends

Kate (*who has been watching her*) You hesitate, Margaret.

Margaret I am afraid—very much afraid of what may befall the Princess and ourselves.

Kate Then you need not come with the rest of us. You heard what the Princess said. She will not reproach you. She will not, now or ever, think the worse of those who stay behind.

Margaret She may not. But, if I stayed here, I would always hate myself. I would never be able to look at myself in the mirror. No, Kate, for good or ill, I go with the others.

Margaret goes out L

Kate watches her departure and sighs

Kate There was never a choice for me. Where she goes, I go—even if it *is* to the Tower.

Kate exits L

The stage is empty for a few moments

Jane the Fool emerges R. *She is the official jester to Queen Mary and she wears a brightly coloured adaptation of the male jester's parti-coloured costume. In her hand she carries a belled bauble and this she flourishes idly as she shambles into view with her back to the audience. She stands looking at the chair, meanwhile, scratching herself reflectively. At length, she turns to face the audience and immediately recoils in seeming horror*

Jane OH! Who are you? Whence came you? WHAT a motley crew! WHAT a shoddy collection of human oddities! How come you to be together in one place? Wait. Wait—I do know you. You are the Commons of England: cruel and kind, miserable and merry, mean and generous, stupid and clever, timid and brave, faithless and true, fraudulent and honest, sour and sweet, inconstant and steadfast. Never was there gathered together in one place such a mingling of vices and qualities! The Commons of England! And most common indeed you look from here! (*She shades her eyes and peers out into the auditorium*) But now that I look again, I do perceive that here and there among you are some of the better sort. Yes, indeed, some there are of gentle blood and some fewer of noble birth. To these latter I do commend myself as Jane the Fool, Jester-in-Ordinary to Queen Mary. (*She looks cautiously off* L *and* R *before confiding*) It is no easy task to be jester to this Queen for I have, thus far, never made her laugh. Never. And you have seen and heard for yourselves that I can readily provoke mirth. But this Queen . . . (*Once more she looks off* L *and* R *before proceeding*) This Queen smiles thinly where another would laugh outright and she frowns like this—(*she illustrates*)—when another person would smile. In short, she is the enemy of mirth and first cousin to misery.

Lady Alicia Mordaunt enters R *just before Jane finishes speaking. She is middle-aged and severe looking. She stands observing Jane*

Alicia With whom do you speak?

Jane Why, with the good folk out there. (*She points in the direction of the audience*)

Alicia (*coming down and looking in the indicated direction*) And who, pray, are they?

Jane Who else but the Commons of England.

Alicia (*turning away in disgust*) The Commons of England are a mindless rabble and no fit company for one who is a member of the royal household. Make yourself scarce, Fool!

Jane (*putting her hands on her hips*) In my own time! In my own time, Lady Alicia!

Alicia This chamber is needed for a conference of your betters. (*She crosses over* L *where she pauses to add threateningly*) You were best gone before I return.

Alicia exits L

Jane (*jerking a thumb in Lady Alicia's direction*) That is Lady Alicia Mordaunt, a Lady-in-Waiting to the Queen and she's just such another as Her Majesty—as merry as a cracked coffin lid.

Mary comes in R. *She checks on seeing Jane, who bobs something between a clumsy bow and an equally clumsy curtsy in the general direction of the Queen*

Give you good morrow, your Majesty.

Mary Good morrow. (*She is guarded in her tone and manner*)

Jane I perceive you are troubled by a royal heir.

Mary I am not troubled, Jane. I would have thought a royal air becoming to one in my situation.

Jane You evade my meaning, your Majesty. Are you not greatly troubled by a royal heir in the person of the Princess Elizabeth?

Mary That is true. But this is not a matter for discussion with a Fool.

Jane Ah, but if the Fool saw the Queen about to play the Fool may not the Fool advise the Queen as if she, the Fool, were Queen?

Mary On this one occasion. But I think it best to warn you, Jane . . .

Jane Do not confuse me with warnings, your Majesty, for, if I see that I have earned your royal displeasure, I will claim Fool's Pardon.

Mary As you wish—Fool's Pardon, it is. But be brief for I am committed.

Jane Then it seems to me that there are two ways of dealing with the Princess Elizabeth. First, you could have her put to death, but that would not serve.

Mary Would it not?

Jane No. The Commons of England would rise up against you for she is very dear to them.

Mary She is?

Jane Very dear. Second, you could bring her to Court, make much of her and treat her as your acknowledged heir.

Mary (*dangerously calm*) To what end? To what end, Fool?

Jane Why, marry, this would please the Commons of England. The Princess is greatly beloved by them.

Mary (*angrily*) You do well to claim Fool's Pardon. Had you not done so . . . (*She breaks off*)

Lady Alicia enters L

Yes. What trouble now?

Alicia No trouble, your Majesty. But the Princess Elizabeth has been waiting to be received this long time past.

Mary Then it will do her no harm to wait a still longer time.

Alicia Your Majesty. (*She curtsies and turns to go*)

Mary No, stay.

Alicia pauses

Admit her when you see this Fool leave the chamber.

Alicia As your Majesty pleases.

Alicia exits L

Mary turns again to Jane

Mary As for you, hear this and take good heed: I did not, after much striving, become Queen of this realm to please the Commons of England. Now go and do not let me see your face again this day!

Jane (*making her awkward obeisance and speaking in imitation of Alicia*) As your Majesty pleases. (*Then, in her normal voice*) With the greatest possible respect, your Majesty, I believe, all things considered, that I would rather be Fool than Queen.

Mary Since the choice is not yours, perhaps it is just as well. (*Pointing*) Now go!

Jane scurries off R

She is dear to the people—is beloved by them. And I am not!

Alicia enters L. She precedes Elizabeth into the chamber. Both women pause as Alicia announces

Alicia The Princess Elizabeth, your Majesty.

With a wave of her hand, Mary dismisses Alicia

Alicia leaves after curtsying to the Queen

Elizabeth advances two or three paces towards Mary and then curtsies deeply. Mary comes over to her, takes her hand and raises her up

Mary So . . . You are come at last, Elizabeth. You have taken your time in answering my summons.

Elizabeth Your Majesty is surely aware that I have been ill—too ill to travel. We were forced to make the journey by easy stages.

Mary Easy stages! I'll warrant they were easy stages! Short journeys and long rests! And do you know why, mistress? Because you were afraid to face your accusers. (*She withdraws and glares at Elizabeth*) That is why you delayed to come to Whitehall!

Elizabeth Your Majesty, I have been truly ill. Your own physician——

Mary (*interrupting*) Pah! (*With a sweep of the hand she dispels the idea of sickness as an excuse*) If you suffered an indisposition—I say if—it was caused by fear of the consequences of your actions.

Elizabeth Neither by word nor deed have I been untrue to your Majesty.

Mary That we shall see. That we shall see. I am informed otherwise.

Elizabeth Then, with respect, your information is false. I understood that I was brought here to be examined by Commissioners. But you speak of accusers. Of what am I accused?

Mary Of complicity in the late rebellion. Of correspondence with the traitor, Wyatt.

Elizabeth Does Wyatt say that I corresponded with him?

Mary He denies it.

Elizabeth Then there is no case for me . . .

Mary But then, he would lie to protect you, his principal. Though he dies, his hope, his prayer, will be that the next uprising will set you on the Throne.

Elizabeth Your Majesty, when you consented to give me an audience, I believed that you would allow me to present my case, to tell you that I am wholly innocent of bearing any part in the late rebellion. It would seem, from what you say, that I am prejudged and found guilty before the enquiry begins.

Mary Oh, you shall have justice, never fear.

Elizabeth I am relieved to hear it. Before God, I say to you that your Majesty has no truer subject, none more devoted, none more loyal.

Elizabeth curtsies. Mary waits until she is once more erect

Mary (*sarcastically*) Bravely said! But you would say as much if you were guilty. All those condemned have made fervent protestations of their loyalty to me but such expressions come a little late in the day after they have appeared in arms against me.

Elizabeth seems about to speak; Mary checks her with upraised hand

No more. I have great confidence in the Commissioners. Let us leave them to decide your innocence or guilt. I had my own reason for granting you this audience.

Elizabeth For whatever reason, I am grateful, your Majesty.

Mary Do not speak too soon of gratitude. Who are you? What is your expectation? What is your title?

Elizabeth Your Majesty knows well my situation and title.

Mary I know, but I fear you do not. You believe yourself to be the Princess Elizabeth and the undoubted heir to the Throne of England.

Elizabeth In your Majesty's view, I am no such thing.

Mary (*echoing*) No such thing. This is my reason for seeing you today: when I was proclaimed Queen, Parliament and the Council of State revoked the divorce of my mother and my father, King Henry the Eighth. This means that all our father's other marriages are to be considered illegal. This means that you are—you are . . .

Elizabeth (*steadily*) Yes, madam? What am I? I beg you, of your kindness, to inform me.

Mary In view of this Act of Revocation, you are declared illegitimate——

Elizabeth (*interrupting*) Illegitimate!

Mary —and therefore, you can have no claim to the Crown of England. I wished to spare you this knowledge. I have, in fact, purposely kept it from you but the possibility that you were linked with Wyatt has forced me to reveal this—unpleasant truth.

Elizabeth For whatever reason, I am grateful to your Majesty for imparting this information. It provides proof, if proof were needed, that my enemies have been most busy while I have been living in—enforced retirement.

Mary You are wrong to lay the blame on your enemies. You must know that, in the Catholic faith, divorce, except by rare dispensation by His Holiness the Pope, is not recognized. Therefore, as this realm now returns to the old faith, King Henry's five later so-called marriages are declared invalid.

Elizabeth Then his marriage to Jane Seymour is alike invalid. The child of that marriage, our brother, the gracious Prince Edward, King Edward the Sixth, is, therefore, like myself, declared illegitimate. Your Majesty, the Council and Parliament have done a grievous wrong to proclaim a King of England bastard.

Mary (*shaken*) I had no part in this. It was the Council and Parliament . . .

Elizabeth Your Majesty is altogether too modest. I am sure that your influence was at work.

Mary You would do well, in your situation, to guard your tongue.

Elizabeth It seems to me, your Majesty, that I have little to lose. I am, I truly believe, accused and condemned before I am examined by your Majesty's Commissioners. I am but a prisoner and you are an all-powerful Queen——

Mary (*interrupting*) You were best to remember that!

Elizabeth —an all-powerful Queen, but I am glad that I have it not on my conscience that I had a hand in bastardizing an annointed King of England. This is something the Commons of England will never forgive you.

Mary (*angrily*) I care nothing for the Commons of England!

Elizabeth Let us hope, your Majesty, there comes not a day when they care nothing for you.

Mary I perceive that I waste time in trying to warn you of the danger in which you stand. There is but one more thing . . .

Elizabeth Ah, with your Majesty there is ever one more thing.

Mary (*furiously*) Impertinence will not serve your cause! Heed this—and heed it well! Now that you have been declared illegitimate, you have no place in the order of precedence and your title of Princess is yours by courtesy only.

Elizabeth A circumstance of which, no doubt, your Majesty will shortly take full advantage.

Mary I am sorely tempted to do so. But I am, in all things, a Christian Queen and have no wish to add to the dangers and troubles which now beset you.

Elizabeth A truly Christian and forbearing Queen.

Mary I thought you should know, before you face the Commissioners, of how matters stand in relation to yourself and the Throne. You have no claim, no rank entitling you to any degree of precedence in royal procession.

Elizabeth A considerate Queen as well as a forbearing and Christian one.

Mary Clearly, your intent is to mock me. But a day may come when you may speak the words in earnest. It is time for you to attend the enquiry. The audience is over.

Elizabeth Then it remains for me to thank you for granting it. I have been instructed and enlightened.

Mary I could wish that, for once, you spoke truly. (*She turns to leave*)

Elizabeth curtsies

Mary goes out R

Elizabeth gazes after her. Her assurance ebbs visibly, and she looks troubled and afraid

Elizabeth Declared illegitimate! Proclaimed a bastard! Now am I truly cast out and rejected. Who would now support my cause?

Alicia enters L. *She curtsies to Elizabeth*

Alicia Your royal Highness, I am to conduct you to the Council Chamber.

Elizabeth (*stonily*) I am ready. (*But she does not move*)

Alicia Your royal Highness . . .

Elizabeth (*guardedly*) Yes?

Alicia Not all of us in this Palace of Whitehall are ill-disposed to you. Please to remember that and take heart.

Alicia goes out L

Elizabeth This Palace of Whitehall is full of surprises.

Elizabeth follows Alicia from the chamber. The four Ladies-in-Waiting enter R *with disciplined gait and bearing. There is something baleful, portentous in their appearance as they stand in line facing the audience*

Emma (*looking upward*) This Council Chamber is vast and vaulted.

Rose The light of day creeps in fearfully through barred windows.

Margaret Listen now! You can hear the reverberations of bygone enquiries.

Nell Listen still! You can hear the echoes of verdicts passed upon prisoners doomed to a terrible death.

Emma Here are gathered together the most cunning lawyers, the most astute Ministers, in all the realm.

Rose So skilled in confusing their victims, the poor fools dig their own graves.

Margaret They are assisted by the most wily prelates in the whole of the Church.

Nell Who can quote you a Bible text to justify anything from mere imprisonment to drawing and quartering.

Emma These ten men, pillars of Church and State, great in office,

Rose Are led by the Lord Chancellor, Stephen Gardiner, sometime Bishop of Winchester,

Margaret A Prince of the Church, with all the graces, all the clemency, all the compassion

Nell Of a hanging-judge.

Emma All these are sworn to try and condemn

Rose A poor princess who, distracted, distraught and distressed

Margaret Knows nothing whereof she is accused

Nell And has but her wit and integrity to oppose them.

The four draw closer together and intone

Emma She is one against ten,

Rose And they are ten to one.

Margaret Oh, what chance has she?

Nell Answer: she has none.

The four now move so that they form a hollow square

Emma This was the way of it. You shall see for yourselves. Let the seat for the accused be set in place.

Rose and Nell detach themselves from the group, move in step to the dais, pick up a stool between them and are bringing it down stage when Emma points to a central spot and commands

There!

They set down the stool and resume their former places. The summons is louder with each repetition

Summon the Princess Elizabeth!
Rose The Princess Elizabeth!
Margaret The Princess Elizabeth!
Nell The Princess Elizabeth!

Elizabeth enters slowly L. *She halts by the stool and faces the front.*

Emma I trust that your Royal Highness is aware of the reason for the summons to appear before this Commission.
Elizabeth It might be in your best interest and mine if you were to state it.
Emma Then it is this: you are accused of being implicated in the late rebellion against Her Majesty the Queen, her Crown and dignity.
Elizabeth This I deny absolutely.
Rose Do you know the traitor, Thomas Wyatt?
Elizabeth I—I have seen him.
Margaret Ah then, you admit that he is known to you.
Elizabeth By sight only. Once at Court he bowed to me.
Nell Have you ever spoken with him?
Elizabeth Never. I have never spoken with him in my life.
Emma And yet he has written to you?
Elizabeth Sequestered as I am, I am in no position to prevent people from writing to me.
Rose Correspondence argues acquaintance.
Elizabeth You are, my lord, in error. He wrote to me. I did not reply. Correspondence lies in interchange—not in a single letter.
Margaret Why did Wyatt write to you?
Elizabeth That is something I cannot answer. You were best to ask Wyatt.
Nell Have no fear. We shall do so, mistress. We shall do so.
Emma There were others in the conspiracy—men more highly placed than Wyatt.
Elizabeth So I have been told.
Rose There was, for instance, the Duke of Suffolk who lately paid the price of his treachery.
Margaret Did you, at any time, hold communication with him?
Elizabeth I did not—nor with any of the other conspirators. Before you all and before God, I tell you plainly that I am no traitor but as faithful a subject of Queen Mary as any of you who today sit in judgement on me.
Nell Our impression is otherwise.
Emma Where does your royal Highness stand on the doctrine of Transubstantiation?

Elizabeth stands with down-bent head with her hands clasped before her

Rose Do you truly believe that the bread and wine are miraculously changed into the body and blood of our Lord, Jesus Christ?
Emma Answer!
Rose Answer!
Margaret Answer!
Nell Answer!

All Answer! Answer! Do you truly believe?

Slowly, Elizabeth raises her head and gazes steadily before her—at her accusers

Elizabeth Christ was the word that spake it;
    He took the bread and brake it;

Her hands go through the motions of breaking bread

    And what His Word did make it,
    That I believe and take it.

She mimes the taking of the bread from her cupped hands

Margaret You deal equivocally with us, mistress.

Nell You answer us with riddles.

Rose As you have done from the start of these proceedings.

Emma We would advise your royal Highness, for your own good, to throw yourself on the Queen's mercy and to seek her pardon.

Elizabeth I shall not do so—now or ever. You waste your breath with me, my lord.

Emma So it would seem. Advice is thrown away on you.

Elizabeth To throw myself upon the Queen's mercy would be a confession of guilt. Pardon in that sort is for the guilty and I will have none of it.

Rose We have been at pains to do our duty to the Queen

Margaret And, at the same time, to be helpful to you.

Nell But you have answered us always with a forked tongue

Emma And defied our efforts to come at the truth.

Rose Have you any request to make before we consider your case in private?

Elizabeth I beg that I may be granted audience with the Queen in order that I may tell her how cruelly I am misused and misinterpreted.

Nell That I can in no wise promise you. Is there anything else you would care to ask? Or to tell us?

Elizabeth To ask? To ask . . .? (*She looks slowly around them and then shakes her head*) No. There is no pity, no understanding in any face before me. To tell you? (*She kindles*) Oh, yes. I wrote with my diamond ring some words on a window—a window in the hall. You were best to read them, my lords Commissioners. You may find those words of interest.

Emma It may be that we shall read them. Now, if you will withdraw, we shall confer and presently make known our deliberations.

Elizabeth As your lordships please. I charge you to remember that, in English law, guilt has to be proved. The onus of proof is on you. All of you and English justice itself are on trial as I am.

Elizabeth curtsies to L *and* R, *and goes out* L

The four draw together again

Emma She was most—apt in her replies. She was not to be shaken.

Rose She is subtle and skilful in her use of words.

Margaret We could not, on the basis of this enquiry, commit her to the Tower.

Nell It would be best if some one of us were to keep the lady closely guarded, closely watched, in his own home.

Emma Would you be the one to undertake the duty? To keep the Queen's sister closely guarded, closely watched? Would you?

Nell Not I, my Lord Chancellor.

Emma Or you, my lord?

Margaret Not I, my Lord Chancellor.

Emma What says your Grace?

Rose Not I, my Lord Chancellor.

Emma Then we must needs, for the safety of this realm, commit her to the Tower. There is still one thing that troubles me.

Rose Yes, my lord?

Emma What is it she has written upon this window pane? Do one of you go and see.

Rose At once, my lord.

Rose goes out L

Emma I shall myself draw up the warrant and see it executed. But first I must see the Queen and report the findings of this Commission. She will not, I think, be pleased with our efforts.

Rose returns

Well, what has she written?

Rose So please you, a sort of rhyme, my lord. It runs:
  "Much suspected, by me
   Nothing proved can be,
   Quoth Elizabeth, prisoner."

Emma Did I not say she was apt? She has summed the matter up better than I could. But I promise you that I shall not quote her to Her Majesty. Come your ways. Our business here is done.

Emma, Rose, Margaret and Nell go out R. Lady Alicia enters L, sees the audience and comes forward. She adopts a confidential manner

Alicia You will wonder why all people, whatever their station, speak of the Tower of London with dread. They are right to do so. This place was built five hundred years ago for William the Conqueror. It has served as a palace, a fortress and a prison. It has been successively strengthened by the sovereigns who followed William. Those same sovereigns have used the Tower as a convenient stronghold in which to imprison those who offended, those who might offend or those who, in any way, might threaten the peace and dignity of Majesty. Many of them lie buried hereabouts. (*She points out front*) There is the Bloody Tower where the young princes, sons of Edward the Fourth, were murdered. (*Pointing off L*) Here gapes Traitor's Gate. Few who pass through this terrifying portal long survive the experience. And it is to this place that the Princess Elizabeth has been committed. (*She shudders*) I entreat your prayers for her. Most assuredly, she has mine. (*She looks off* R) This is not a place to linger. Give you good day.

Alicia curtsies briefly and goes out R. *Almost at once, Kate Ashley, wearing a cloak, enters* R. *She has seen Alicia in passing and glances back over her shoulder as if watching that lady's departure. Then she advances, looking apprehensively about her*

Kate This is no place for her. This is most truly no place for my mistress. (*Looking up*) And it rains! How it rains!

Elizabeth, also cloaked, enters R. *She moves forward reluctantly, halts and points out front*

Elizabeth What! Are all those harnessed men here for me?

Kate No, no. No such thing.

Elizabeth They are—and well you know it. Nothing is ever made better by lies however well-meaning. (*To the assembled soldiery*) You are brave men to come thus in arms against a few defenceless women. (*To Kate*) What place is this?

Kate (*hesitantly*) My dear lady—I cannot—cannot bring myself . . .

Elizabeth You were best to tell me else I shall ask one of these. (*She flourishes a hand in the general direction of the guards*) No doubt they would be happy to tell me.

Kate Then, your royal Highness, over there is Traitor's Gate. (*She indicates*) Indeed, we stand in its very shadow.

Elizabeth Do we so? Then hear me, all of you! Here stands as true a subject, being prisoner, as ever stood in the shadow of Traitor's Gate. I tell you this I shall not pass through it unless you drag me by force, and who is he who will lay a hand upon a princess of Tudor blood?

Kate Sweet mistress, I beg you to come in with me out of the rain.

Elizabeth (*as if Kate had not spoken*) This, for me, is a haunted place. It is so short a time since here they did to death my sweet cousin, Jane Grey. (*She moves a little and points*) Here is where they cut off the head of Thomas Seymour, a man of much wit and very little judgement— yet one who loved me well. (*She moves a little further and points again*) Here it was that my own mother—(*she breaks off and is momentarily overcome*)—my own mother met a violent death at my father's command. (*Suddenly, hysterically*) Tell me, my masters, am I brought here to keep company with my dead?

Kate Peace! Peace! You do no good to any—least of all to yourself!

Kate seeks to restrain the princess, but Elizabeth fends her off

Elizabeth Hear me again! Oh Lord, I never thought to have come in as prisoner; and I pray you all, good friends and fellows, bear me witness that I come as no traitor but as true a woman to the Queen's Majesty as any now living and thereon will I take my death. (*She goes over to the* *stool and sits, adding more quietly*) And I will sit here upon this stone for ever if need be but I will not pass through Traitor's Gate.

Kate Nay, madam, do not sit there unwholesomely in the rain.

Elizabeth You look bedraggled, Kate.

Kate It is very likely, your royal Highness.

Elizabeth And you are exceeding wet, Kate.

Kate That, too, your royal Highness.

Elizabeth And you look cold, Kate.

Kate I am indeed very cold, your royal Highness.

Elizabeth Then do you go inside out of the cold and the rain.

Kate That I may not well do unless your royal Highness goes also.

Elizabeth You are a very difficult, stubborn woman, Kate.

Kate They tell me that I have much in common with your royal Highness.

Elizabeth You are wet and cold and old. Give me your hand, Kate.

Kate does so and helps her to her feet

We shall go within if only so that you may be spared the cold and the rain.

Kate moves as if to pass through the gate in advance of the Princess, but Elizabeth restrains her

No, no. Give place. I claim my right of precedence. I am the true Heir-Apparent. Only the Queen herself may go through that gate ahead of me.

Erect and regal, the Princess Elizabeth passes through Traitor's Gate. Kate follows her; they exit L. *Zuleika Daniels enters* R. *She is a slatternly, ill-dressed woman, dark, middle-aged, slovenly and none too clean. Round her waist she wears a belt from which a bunch of large keys is suspended. She looks about her with a gloating expression*

Zuleika And it is the Princess Elizabeth herself who is to be shut up in this hole! (*She cackles*) Why, I am better lodged myself. Yes, and I'll be better fed though I am but the widow of a guard and maintained here on sufferance. Princess! That means she's used to dainty fare, rare wines, perfumes, soft beds with silk sheets, with music and company for the asking. Yes, and those to fetch and carry, to go here and go there and do her instant bidding. Oh, she'll get short shrift here! She'll get rough fodder, hard lying and such service as *I* consider she should have. But she will be grateful for that which I do for her. Grateful and generous if she is sensible of her situation. I'll have her begging for favours! (*Holding out her hand*) I'll have her eating out of this hand! I'll do nothing beyond provision of the bare necessities without recompense. Oh, I shall do rarely out of this high-born madam. Pray God that they are in no hurry to behead her!

Elizabeth, still cloaked, enters L *towards the end of Zuleika's speech and stands observing her*

Zuleika turns and is startled to see Elizabeth—but she quickly recovers

Elizabeth And who are you?

Zuleika Ah, that's where I am at vantage. I know you—the Princess Elizabeth.

Elizabeth Then, if you know who I am, you should do me courtesy.

Zuleika Courtesy? To you? (*She laughs ironically*) Who do you think you are? I'll tell you—you are but a prisoner here confined perhaps for your natural term else to be taken from here to the block and beheaded.

Elizabeth It may be that you are right, but are you one who takes advantage of the unfortunate and defenceless in this place?

Zuleika Yes, I am such a one and you would do well to recognize it. Your rank, your blood, your connections, mean nothing here! Nothing to me! You were best to see me well provided for if you wish for me to provide you with comforts and food that you can eat.

Elizabeth Clearly, you know nothing of me or you would not seek to intimidate me. I do not yield to threats.

Zuleika We shall see what you have to say when you have been here for a week on maggoty meat, mouldy bread and slimy water. Then we shall have a different answer.

Elizabeth As you say. In the meantime, I shall have written to my sister, the Queen.

Zuleika (*laughing uproariously*) They all do that! They all start by telling me of their high-born kindred. Your sister, the Queen, must have thought well of you when she committed you to this place. You will not frighten me with your talk of Queens and letters. I took care of the Lady Jane Grey.

Elizabeth I am sure she was appreciative of your kindly ministrations.

Zuleika She made a brave end, the little one.

Elizabeth Then I hope I shall do as well if I am called upon to do so.

Zuleika inspects Elizabeth judiciously from different angles

Zuleika Yes, you would, I do believe. I can always tell which ones will . . . (*She breaks off, regarding Elizabeth with something between fear and amazement. When she speaks, she sounds frightened*) I never saw the like before! What is it?

Elizabeth What ails you, woman?

Zuleika (*shielding her eyes*) The light!

Elizabeth (*bewildered*) It is dark in here—quite dark.

Zuleika It dazzles! (*She drops on her knees before Elizabeth*) Forget what I said. Please forget. Forgive a poor gipsy.

Elizabeth Forget? Forgive?

Zuleika On your brow—about your head—the signs are there. Lady you are greatly blessed. (*She gets to her feet*) Sit down. Please sit down.

Elizabeth does as she is bidden

Give me your hand. (*She kneels and studies Elizabeth's palm at great length and then looks up with an ecstatic expression*) Let not the miseries of this present season overcast your spirits. There is a time, not far away, when all will be changed, upon the instant. I see you robed in splendour, riding in a golden coach. You are waving to a cheering crowd, and bells are pealing joyfully.

Elizabeth Then I am . . .

Zuleika You are to be such a Prince as will stir the hearts and minds of all men. You shall be remembered when lesser Princes are dust in their tombs. I see glory, only glory.

Elizabeth And happiness? Do you see happiness for me?

Zuleika (*shaking her head*) The glory outshines all else.

Elizabeth (*nodding*) Well enough. Then I must be well content with glory.

She starts to rise, but Zuleika hugs her round the knees and prevents her

Zuleika Forgive me. Forgive me, Princess. I did not know you. Forgive the words I spoke.

Elizabeth We all use hard words and threats betimes. Myself in particular, for I am like my father and have a rough tongue. Now let me go.

Zuleika releases her. Elizabeth rises

If so be that you saw truly . . .

Zuleika Upon my life, your Grace, I promise you . . .

Elizabeth No more. Leave be. I still do not know your name.

Zuleika Mistress Daniels, widow, your Grace. I'm called Zuleika. I am but a sort of gaoler here, but from henceforth I am your devoted servant— if you will have me.

Elizabeth Mine is a very small establishment—at present.

Zuleika Give me your cloak. I will dry it by the fire. (*She takes the cloak and starts to leave* R)

Elizabeth Stay! Am I not obliged by custom to cross your palm with silver?

Zuleika Keep your silver, Princess. I will wait until your time is come when you may give me gold—with your image stamped thereon.

Zuleika goes out R

Elizabeth moves forward, deep in thought

Elizabeth ". . . robed in splendour. In a golden coach . . ." God grant it! ". . . gold, with my image stamped thereon." God grant it—soon.

Zuleika returns without the cloak

Zuleika Mistress, would you come within? There is a fire to warm you and I can make you a hot posset.

With a courteous gesture at odds with her appearance, Zuleika indicates the room beyond and Elizabeth goes within. Zuleika follows. After a moment, Rose peeps out R and then emerges stealthily. She tip-toes with several backward glances to the centre of the chamber. Here she pauses, looks back and beckons. Margaret enters and approaches Rose with equal caution. She halts and the two girls stand face to face. Both place finger-

tips to lips, make a shushing noise and, in unison, look behind them to ensure that they are not overheard

Margaret I have news.
Rose Tell me your news.

Margaret glances around for reassurance

Margaret It concerns—Philip of Spain.
Rose Oh, please tell!
Margaret (*with, once again, the backward glance*) He has married Queen Mary by proxy!
Rose Oh, no! By proxy!
Margaret Yes, another man stood up in the church and married Queen Mary in place of Philip of Spain.
Rose Do you know what I would do if I were Philip of Spain?
Margaret Oh, please tell!

Now Rose is the one to dart a furtive backward glance

Rose Taking into account the Queen's well-known sour disposition——
Margaret Y—e—s?

Both look fearfully behind them and then, emboldened, turn to face one another again

Rose —and her famous uncertain temper——
Margaret Y—e—s?
Rose —coupled with her conspicuous lack of charm——
Margaret Y—e—s?
Rose —I would leave the proxy to carry out ALL—and I mean ALL—the conditions of the marriage contract!

They squeal with laughter and cover their mouths with their hands. Then, startled at their own temerity, they run from the chamber

Margaret and Rose exit L

The stage is briefly empty, and a few bars of music are played to establish an atmosphere of dread and menace

Elizabeth enters R. She looks troubled, and makes her way to the dais and disconsolately sits on the chair. Emma and Nell come on R, and Margaret and Rose L. They form into line facing the front. As Emma begins to speak, the music fades

Emma Now is this realm of England plunged into a deep despondency of spirit.
Rose In the name of Christ one brother betrays another to his death.
Margaret In the market place and at the gallowsfoot, the fires are lit.
Nell And God's faithful die terribly in the flames.
Emma Our Queen is wed with Philip of Spain.
Rose It is Spain which now rules this Commonwealth.
Margaret Spain and the Holy See of Rome,
Nell Which, in the Pope's name, forbids tolerance, denies liberty
Emma And promotes tyranny and oppression throughout this land.

Rose All this in the name of Christ, the Redeemer,
Margaret Christ, the Lamb of God,
Nell Christ, the Prince of Peace,
Emma Christ, the Prophet of Love.
Rose Now are the people of this realm
Margaret Shaken in their faith,
Nell Utterly broken in spirit,
Emma Betrayed by those in whom they trusted,
Rose Helpless in the face of constituted authority,
Margaret And so cowed are they by restrictions,
Nell So confused by new laws and prohibitions,
Emma That they are crushed,
Rose Beaten,
Margaret Destroyed,
Nell Defeated
Emma And dispossessed.
All (*as if repeating a psalm*) Let us grieve for the passing of the shining
   heritage of a proud nation. Let us mourn that the bright traditions of
   a once-great people lie today in the trampled dust.

*They stand with bowed heads. Elizabeth has been listening with obvious
distress. Her expression is protest made manifest. Now she rises slowly but
with an air of purpose*

Elizabeth (*at the top of her voice*) NO! Lift up your heads!

They do so

   No! You are grievously mistaken! This is not a beaten people, not a
   defeated nation! These English will endure tyranny and oppression for
   a season until they see no hope of relief. Then are they most dangerous
   to the tyrant and the oppressor, for then endurance will have an end
   and they will rise up in their wrath and will know no rest, no repose,
   until the oppressor is swept away, the tyrant cast down. So let the
   King of Spain, let the Pope of Rome, make the most of what little time
   is left to them for soon, soon, comes the hour of their overthrow. This
   I say to you: if it shall be my good fortune to lead these English out of
   bondage to Spain and Rome, I shall know myself to be blessed beyond
   deserving for, leading such a people how can I fail to win a bright place
   in history?

*Elizabeth leaves the dais and, moving as in a trance, she halts in front of
her ladies and faces the audience. It is growing ever darker but it seems that
now we see the radiance which captivated Zuleika. It surrounds Elizabeth
and is brightest about her head*

   Rouse up! Rouse up! And, at your bravest and best, you may prove
   worthy of these English! To serve such a people, I dedicate myself,
   heart and mind, body and soul!

Exalted, Elizabeth stands erect with the brightness surrounding her, as—

the CURTAIN *falls*

ACT II

The scene is as before. The four Ladies-in-Waiting are already drawn up in line in front of the dais

Emma The Queen and Philip of Spain are wed at last
Rose With resounding pomp and due ceremony
Margaret When the Cathedral of Winchester was hung with cloth of gold.
Nell Now is the Queen full of love and pride for her husband.
Emma He is, after all, a proper man, of fine presence,
Rose Of good address, given to flattering speeches,
Margaret Turns of phrase and expressions of goodwill.
Nell And love? Did he, at any time, speak of love?
Emma You ask too much. This is, after all,
Rose A marriage of convenience and one which, it is hoped,
Margaret Will provide England with a Catholic dynasty.
Nell And we have a question for you.
Emma It is:
All Do any of you find Queen Mary lovable?
Margaret Still, still, does terror stalk this land
Nell With so-called heretics dragged from their homes,
Emma Flung into verminous prisons,
Rose Delivered to summary judgement
Margaret And condemned to a hideous death.
Nell Oh, England! How long shall be this night
Emma Lit redly by the pyres of burning saints?
Rose The Commons of England suffer and endure,
Margaret Suffer and endure comforting themselves
Nell With something between a jingle and a prayer.
Emma It is:
All Out of despair, darkness and death,
  Pray, God, send us our Elizabeth.
Emma And what of the Princess
Rose Forlorn hope of the Commons of England?
Margaret She did not attend the wedding
Nell Though it was otherwise legal in every particular!
Emma How wise, how very wise, was the Queen
Rose Not to invite our Princess to the celebration of the nuptials
Margaret For who would perceive the lanthorn's glow
Nell In the full blaze of the noonday sun?
Emma No, the Princess is still in the Tower,
Rose Still sore beset by calculating Commissioners
Margaret Who visit her at intervals

Nell In the hope that the provoked, unwary answer
Emma May yet provide them with
Rose The semblance of guilt.
Margaret She now returns from such a session.
Nell But no longer is she subservient to these inquisitors.
Emma She turns their own questions upon them,
Rose Meets their wiles with smart stratagems
Margaret And confounds their dry legalities
Nell With apt answers and ready rejoinders.

They all look expectantly towards the entrance L

Elizabeth comes in

They all curtsy, Elizabeth pausing as they do so

Emma You are early returned, Princess.
Rose This was but a brief session, your royal Highness.
Elizabeth Because I chose to end it when I did. I could no longer endure
   to return the accustomed answer to the oft-repeated questions. (*She
   draws herself erect and re-enacts the exchange with the Commissioners*)
   I said to them: "I marvel that men of your standing in this realm can
   come here, time after time, and speak of treason to Great Harry's
   daughter. Before God, my masters, I would my father were here for
   just two minutes. In that short space he would show us how to deal
   with a scurvy, ill-conditioned, ill-assorted collection of hair-splitting
   lawyers and mealy-mouthed, hypocritical clerics!"
All four Ladies-in-Waiting register varying degrees of shock

Margaret Oh, Princess! You do harm to your cause!
Nell And what followed?
Elizabeth Three of them rushed forward to kiss my hand and a fourth
   burst into tears. For all their show of threat and bluster, there are those
   among them who are no more than a pack of old women.
Emma Then have you done with the Commissioners, Princess?
Elizabeth I have been done with them this long time past. But they have
   not done with me.
Emma There will be more sessions?
Elizabeth It may well be that there will be more sessions. There are those
   of the Commissioners that I can move to pity and those in whom I
   can arouse a generosity of spirit. But there is still the Lord Chancellor.
   I watched him closely today. I did not reach him. I never shall. There is a
   man who truly hates me.
Margaret Oh no, Princess.
Elizabeth Who truly hates me. But I shall be spared his company for a little
   while. I am summoned by the Queen.
Margaret That, surely, is good news.
Elizabeth It could be good—or bad. But, strangely, Kate Ashley is also
   summoned—separately. Now why is this? What do they hope to learn
   from her? I can tell them now. Nothing.
Nell You speak of "they", your royal Highness. Who are "they"?

Elizabeth Why, the Lord Chancellor and his minions. They are forever
there in the background—advising the Queen—dominating her. (*She
muses*) Kate Ashley . . . There is menace here. This troubles me. This
troubles me greatly. (*With a change of tone*) But come! We must make
ready.

*The Ladies-in-Waiting follow Elizabeth as she leads the way and all go off
L. Hardly have they done so than Mary enters R, supported by Lady Alicia
and another attendant we have not seen hitherto: Lady Harriet Scrope.
Like Alicia, she is middle-aged and soberly dressed. The two Ladies-in-
Waiting assist the Queen to the dais and ease her solicitously into the
chair. Mary relaxes and sighs*

Harriet Are you comfortable, your Majesty?
Mary No. But I am as much at my ease as I may be at this time. Where
is the woman, Ashley?
Alicia She is in the anteroom, your Majesty. She has been there for some
time.
Mary That is as it should be. She is under guard?
Harriet As you directed, your Majesty.
Mary Then do you, Harriet, bring her here to me. I wish to see her face so
that in future I may recognize a traitor when I see one.

Harriet still lingers

Go, Harriet. Bring her.
Harriet (*going*) At once, your Majesty.

Harriet goes out L

Alicia You are wrong to see this wretched woman, your Majesty. You
should not agitate yourself. I do entreat you . . .
Mary I am well enough and I am determined to see her. Do not trouble
yourself. She, I do assure you, will be the one who is agitated.

*Harriet returns with Kate, who is considerably dishevelled and looks
frightened*

(*As they enter*) So this is that contemptible traitor, Kate Ashley! (*Pointing*) Stand there!

*Kate steps forward hesitantly and halts on the indicated spot. She curtsies
clumsily. Harriet has paused some little way off so that Kate appears iso-
lated. Head on one side, Mary surveys the woman before her*

Lift up your head!

Kate does as she is bidden

Let the light fall on your face. And this is the face of a conspirator. Yes . . .
Yes . . . There is guile, cunning and malice aplenty and over all there is
resentment—envy—hatred. You are a witch, are you not, Kate Ashley?
Kate No, no! I am no such thing, your Majesty!
Mary Yet you did confess as much.

Kate When they tortured me. I am an old woman—I could not bear more. I would then have confessed to anything, your Majesty.

Mary Except that your mistress was involved in your plots.

Kate She knew nothing—nothing of this.

Mary I am much rejoiced that even such as you have one virtue—even if it is only that of misplaced loyalty. So you are a self-confessed witch—one who casts spells and mouths incantations so that I might die and make room for your Princess.

Kate I tell you, as I hope for salvation, that I am no witch, your Majesty.

Mary (*as if she had not spoken*) Casting spells that I might die most painfully. Well, you are the one who will die in lingering torment because, as you well know, we make an—extended ceremony of despatching witches.

Kate Your Majesty, I beg of you . . .

Mary Oh, you beg for mercy now—you who would have shown none. And then there are those books you kept hidden—books which made a mockery of the true faith. Do you deny that you had such books?

Kate (*reluctantly*) I had some books—books that were sent to me.

Mary Why, that is worse than casting spells! You are of that persuasion that I am resolved to root out and destroy. Would you, then, prefer to die as a heretic? Shall we burn you, Mistress Ashley, as we have burned so many of your betters, at the stake?

Kate (*falling on her knees*) Unworthy as I am, I do most abjectly entreat mercy of your Majesty, who is a truly Christian Queen. If you will but extend to me your renowned clemency——

Mary (*interrupting*) Silence! You sicken me, Ashley. I will hear no more of your canting hypocrisy. But I will show you the mercy of a Christian Queen. I will spare you. Upon conditions.

Kate (*rising*) Oh, your Majesty is the most gracious, the most compassionate of sovereigns. I shall ever remember you——

Mary (*interrupting*) Listen! I said there were conditions. You may not feel so grateful when you hear them. They are these: you will leave the service of the Princess Elizabeth forthwith.

Kate (*shrieking*) Oh, no! Not that! Not that! (*She is down on her knees again*) I entreat you in the name of Mary, Mother of God! It is for the Princess's sake as well as mine——

Mary (*interrupting, shouting*) Be silent! Or I shall see that you are put to silence! You will leave the service of the Princess and you are not to see her face again as long as you live. (*She rises*) Get up! Get up from your knees!

Kate does so

You are to remember always that this is something which you provoked by your treachery.

Kate sobs bitterly

I am something touched by your devotion to your mistress else would I have had you put to death as you deserve. Thank God kneeling every night hereafter that I have been so moved.

Kate (*utterly broken and dejected*) Nay, your Majesty! If that is to be the way of it, then take my life. Without the Princess, it has no meaning.

Mary (*regarding her sourly*) You tempt me, mistress. You tempt me sorely. Did you think to escape punishment altogether? (*To Harriet*) Take her away. Turn her over to the guard.

Harriet Yes, your Majesty.

Harriet moves towards Kate but pauses as Mary commands

Mary Wait! They are to put her beyond the confines of this Palace and thence she must find her own way to those who might provide her with food and shelter. If there are any such to be found. Take her.

As Harriet moves towards her, Kate curtsies mechanically

Harriet takes Kate by the arm and leads her off L

Mary watches Kate's melancholy progress until she has passed out of sight. Then she sways and puts her hand to her head. Immediately, Alicia is at her side, supporting her and wearing an expression of concern

Alicia Your Majesty is unwell. I begged you not to see that woman. There was no need.

Mary I had to see her. You know that. I am the better for seeing her.

Alicia (*guiding Mary to the chair*) That I doubt very much. If your Majesty would be pleased to sit . . .

Mary is eased into the chair and sighs deeply. Alicia hovers solicitously. Mary makes an ineffectual effort to wave her away

Mary No, no. It is nothing. It will pass.

Harriet returns. She is at once alarmed by Mary's appearance and halts

Harriet What ails her Majesty?

Alicia She is faint. The cordial—quickly!

Harriet hurriedly retraces her steps and goes out once more L

You must realize, your Majesty, that it is now out of the question for you to see the Princess. I will not be responsible . . .

Mary I must and shall see her.

Alicia Your Majesty, the strain of such an encounter could bring about your death.

Mary Then that is a hazard I must take. You must remember that my lord enjoined me to see her. Indeed he advised me how I must treat with her.

Alicia My lord could not then know that you would be in such distress or that you would be . . . (*She breaks off*)

Harriet returns, bearing a goblet

Alicia takes it from her

You poured the cordial yourself?

Harriet I did. Then I returned the phial to the cupboard which I locked again most carefully.

Alicia nods approval and then holds the goblet to Mary's lips. Mary sips and then sinks back as if exhausted

Mary That is better. It is a brave cordial—heartening—restoring.

Alicia proffers the goblet again. Feebly Mary waves it away

No more. Keep the goblet by.

Alicia I should be failing in my duty, your Majesty, if I did not urge you to give up your intention of seeing the Princess today.

Harriet With your permission, your Majesty, I will see her comfortably lodged and you could see her, when you are rested, tomorrow.

Mary You are good souls and mean well. But, if I were to wait until tomorrow, the Princess might have learned or guessed the reason for my summons. Is she here?

Harriet She is, your Majesty. She waits in the audience chamber.

Mary I will see her here. Once I have spoken to her, I will know peace. (*She muses, corrects herself*) A measure of peace. (*To Harriet*) Come, Harriet. Escort the Princess to our presence.

With a doubtful glance at the Queen, Harriet goes out R

I will take another draught of the cordial.

But she only sips from the goblet when Alicia holds it to her lips

Enough. Put it aside.

Alicia I will do so. (*She places the goblet on the floor*) If your Majesty should feel the need of it . . . (*She breaks off*)

Harriet enters R, *with Elizabeth*

Harriet does not advance far into the chamber, but Elizabeth sweeps forward until she stands before the seated Queen. Then Elizabeth and Harriet curtsy in unison. Mary smiles unpleasantly as she regards Elizabeth

Mary So you come in answer to my summons.

Elizabeth As you see, your Majesty. I am your most obedient servant.

Mary That has yet to be demonstrated.

As Elizabeth seems about to protest, Mary makes a quelling gesture

No matter. Have you any notion as to why I summoned you?

Elizabeth None, your Majesty.

Mary You can advance no speculation? Hazard no guess?

Elizabeth I am, at my best, but an indifferent guesser. Your Majesty must indulge me.

Mary Then I must tell you my news without preamble. I am with child.

Elizabeth With—child? (*She is obviously shaken*)

Mary (*smiling again*) Ah, you change colour. Your eyes are dulled. There is a tremor in your cheek. This was something you did not expect.

Elizabeth (*faltering*) I was not prepared . . . It is just that I am—surprised. I will need some little time to accustom myself . . .

Mary Indeed you will. For this changes everything. Your days as acknowledged heir are numbered.

Elizabeth I had, from our last interview, understood myself to be declared illegitimate.

Mary That was indeed the case, but the Commons of England either did not understand the declaration or they refused to accept it. But even they, clods that they are, must see that your claim to the Throne of England, if you ever had one, is now as nothing—insubstantial—hollow —empty.

Elizabeth It would seem so, your Majesty.

Mary Seem so? Seem so! It is! You are no longer of any consequence. No longer a threat to my peace.

Elizabeth If ever I was, such was not my intent.

Mary (*echoing*) Not your intent . . . How could you be otherwise? With the Commons of England—aye, and many of the nobler sort—your supporters to a man. (*She rises*) Oh, you are beloved because you have those glittering, spurious qualities which catch the eye and stir the imagination of the mindless mob. (*She is becoming increasingly distraught*) You have not the true faith in your heart. You would not, for the good of the realm, burn the unbeliever and the heretic.

Elizabeth Since I am not to reign, your Majesty, surmise is unprofitable.

Mary You have not the true faith at heart. If you ruled, impiety and ungodliness would thrive! (*She has been shouting and has roused herself to a state of excitement. Now, panting, she pauses*)

Elizabeth (*solicitously*) You were best to take care, your Majesty. (*Leaning forward, she looks closely at Mary*) Clearly, you are overwrought. There is a tremor in your cheek.

Mary makes a visible effort at control

Mary You are at some pains to provoke me but I shall not be baited. (*Shouting again*) Do you hear? I shall not be baited!

Elizabeth Yes, your Majesty, I hear you.

Mary And, since I told you that our marriage has been blessed, you have uttered no single word of congratulation. Is it because you find yourself excluded from the succession?

Elizabeth No, your Majesty. I have had little opportunity to compose myself. (*In a flat tone*) But I do felicitate your Majesty and your royal husband. May your child grow up to be a great ruler, wise, strong and greatly loved.

Mary You spoke as if you meant no word of what you said. But no matter—you have uttered the stilted phrases and I have joyed to hear them. It seemed to me as if the words would choke you. I have consulted with my lord as to your future. He is, as all men know, a wise, far-seeing and clement prince.

Elizabeth (*echoing*) As all men know, your Majesty.

Mary My lord maintains that, now you are no longer the heir, there is no need to keep you confined in the Tower.

Elizabeth A clement prince, indeed.

Mary But, so that you are not made the tool of some rebellious faction, you will be housed in some fitting, well-guarded residence at some distance from the Court.

Elizabeth As your Majesty says—a far-seeing prince.

Mary But you will have a smaller retinue as from this time. Kate Ashley will no longer be a member of your household.

Elizabeth Why will she not?

Mary Because she is a proven witch and traitress and, as such, not fitted to have any place in your establishment. I have just received her in audience and told her, upon pain of death, that she must not set eyes on you again. It is in your interest that I have done this.

Elizabeth It is not. You do not understand. She is so much to me—the nearest to a mother that I ever knew. (*She falls upon her knees*) Do not, your Majesty, thus revenge yourself on me. For pity's sake . . .

Mary Get up. It is not meet that a Tudor princess should kneel and entreat pardon for such as Kate Ashley. Get up, I say!

Harriet moves swiftly over to Elizabeth, helps her to rise and then returns to her former position

This audience is at an end. You have our permission to withdraw.

Elizabeth (*entreating*) Your Majesty . . .

Mary (*with increasing chill*) You have our permission to withdraw. Hatfield will be your new home.

Elizabeth curtsies. Alicia supports Mary and helps her to be seated again. Harriet goes over and takes her place beside the chair. Alicia produces the goblet. Mary takes it from her and sits sipping the cordial. Away from the others, Elizabeth seems downcast and lonely

Elizabeth Home—I do but exchange one prison for another. (*She muses unhappily*) And the Queen is to bear a child. (*She laughs bitterly*) So much for the gipsy who saw me riding in a golden coach waving to cheering multitudes.

Mary glances up and sees Elizabeth looking woe-begone

Mary You are something mournful, Elizabeth. Do you lack for mirth in your confinement?

Elizabeth (*wearily*) Your Majesty, I do lack for many things. So do the members of my poor household. Mirth is but one commodity of which I have a most plentiful lack.

Mary Then I shall do my best to amend it. You shall have my Fool.

Elizabeth regards her incredulously. Mary adds reassuringly

Yes, you shall have Jane the Fool to attend on you. At this time I have no need of her.

Elizabeth (*to herself*) Nor I at any time.

Mary makes a sign to Alicia, who comes down to Elizabeth. Mary becomes abstracted and sits staring before her with the goblet cupped in her hands

Alicia I am to conduct your royal Highness.

Elizabeth (*with an attempt at a smile*) Who better for that duty?

Elizabeth is about to go but Alicia detains her by a light touch on the arm

Alicia Could I say that I have great sympathy for your royal Highness? I feel deeply for you in your troubles.

Elizabeth How should you know anything of troubles such as mine?

Alicia One does not have to be a great personage, Princess, to know great troubles.

Elizabeth nods agreement with the observation and follows Alicia out R

Mary emerges from her reverie and looks about her

Mary She has gone? The Princess has gone?

Harriet She left but now with Lady Alicia, your Majesty. Do you wish me to——

Mary (*interrupting*) No, no. (*She hands the goblet to Harriet*) The Princess did not appear to appreciate my offer of Jane the Fool.

Harriet (*acidly*) Jane's fooling is not to the taste of everyone, your Majesty.

Mary Not to yours by your tone of voice.

Harriet It is just that I think men are much more comical. (*She considers*) Much, much more comical. (*She considers further*) Perhaps it is the way that they are made.

Mary It is true that men have a greater talent for making themselves ridiculous. (*She pauses and reflects once more*) It was just that she touched my heart and I could not find the—apt words to say to her. Standing there, she looked as she so often did when she was a child—lost—forlorn—forsaken. Then would I take her up before me on my horse and we would ride round the tiltyard, else would I take her to sit by the fire for she was ever one to feel the cold. (*She sighs*) It may well be that we leave the best of ourselves behind us in our childhood.

Alicia returns. She halts short of the dais and surveys Mary with concern

Alicia Your Majesty looks greatly fatigued.

Mary I am indeed very tired. With your help, I will go and rest. Give me your arm.

Alicia goes to Mary, helps her to rise and takes her arm. Together they leave the dais and begin a slow progress towards the exit R, *with Harriet carrying the goblet, following them. A not-too-distant joyful peal of bells is heard. Mary appears troubled. She halts and so, of course, do the others*

Mary What is that?

Neither reply

Come, what means that peal of bells?

Alicia It is a peal rung by some who favour the Princess Elizabeth, your Majesty.

Harriet They have interpreted your summons as the prelude to her release from the Tower.

Mary (*turning to glare at her*) Have they now?

Harriet (*quailing*) There are those who hold the Princess in high esteem.

Mary A circumstance of which I am only too fully aware. We shall see if they will esteem her as highly when they learn that she is no longer my heir.

They start off again but have gone only a pace or two when Mary halts once more

Mary They shall be set in the pillory.

Alicia Who shall, your Majesty?

Mary Those men who rang the bells without authority. See to it.

Alicia Yes, your Majesty.

There is no further delay, and they all go off R

A moment or two afterwards, the sound of the church bells fades away

The four Ladies-in-Waiting enter L, and face the audience

Emma So the downtrodden Commons of England

Rose Do not celebrate, jubilate or commemorate

Margaret This news of the impending royal birth

Nell For it seems to them that this can but perpetuate——

Rose (*awed*) What word was that?

Nell "Perpetuate"—meaning to cause to last for ever.

Rose (*curtsying*) I thank you. Proceed.

Nell (*with a peevish glance at Rose*)——that this can but perpetuate

Emma A Catholic dynasty which will rule

Rose Over this miserable, stricken land

Margaret From this present time

Nell Until the crack of doom.

Emma There are, it is reported, mountains of infant clothes

Rose Filling two large apartments in the Palace

Margaret And there is a cradle, a cradle royally worked,

Nell Upon which is inscribed a rhyme

Emma So vile,

Rose So ill-executed,

Margaret So ungrammatical,

Emma That lots were drawn

Rose To decide who

Margaret Should recite it.

Nell I lost. Hearken:
"The child which, through Mary, O Lord of Might, has send
    To England's joy, in health, preserve, keep and defend."

(*She puts her hand to her mouth and darts scared glances at the audience*)

I cry you mercy and beg all your several pardons. (*She curtsies*)

Emma Would that we had that rhymer here
Rose So that we might reprimand him,
Margaret So that we might reason with him
Nell And cut off his writing hand.
Emma And what can we do in this lamentable situation?
Rose We who see the hopes, the dreams and the aspirations
Margaret Of our Princess and the Commons of England
Nell Come to naught.
Emma We can but pray and this we do.

All kneel except Emma, who looks Heavenwards

Thou knowest, Lord, from our last communication, what it is we ask of Thee.

Emma kneels beside the others. All clasp their hands and offer up this prayer

All O God, we be but four poor maids
Who, praying, ask from you a boon:
We beg you send a miracle
And pray, God, send it soon.

The Lights black-out for a few moments and, when the stage is lit again, all four Ladies-in-Waiting have gone

Jane the Fool enters R, *cautiously and somewhat unsteadily. She peers off* L, *is intimidated by what she sees and backs out again. Zuleika comes on* L. *She is neater, cleaner and altogether more brisk than when we saw her last and there is, too, about her that touch of authority to be found in some servants in royal households. She takes first one stool and then the other, removes them from the dais and sets them in juxtaposition so that one can serve as a seat and the other as a table. Head on one side, she surveys the arrangement, makes a minor adjustment and goes out* L. *In a moment, she returns with a tray which she places on the table/stool. Upon the tray is an assortment of food—later dealt with in detail—a large goblet of wine and an equally large tankard of beer. She has just set down the tray when she hears a noise and looks off to trace the source of it. When it seems that she has done so, she moves forward a pace or two, places her hands on her hips and calls out*

Zuleika You there! Jane! I see you! Come out! Come out now!

Jane emerges looking shamefaced

What are you doing there?
Jane I was—I was keeping out of the way.
Zuleika And I know why—you have been at the Harvest ale again.
Jane (*indignantly*) No such thing!
Zuleika (*threateningly*) Jane!
Jane Well—just a pot or two to keep out the cold.
Zuleika (*puzzled*) But it is not cold.
Jane Then I am well prepared for a change of weather.

Zuleika If you were as adept at fooling as you are at eating and drinking, you would be the greatest clown in the whole world.

Jane And I am none so badly placed that am Fool to the Queen of England. What are you that would look down on such as me?

Zuleika I will tell you. I am a sometime gaoler taken by the Princess into her service. I serve her as something between a scullion and a body servant. This I am proud to do for she is a great personage and shall be greater still.

Jane Will she so? That is still to be seen. (*She indicates the tray*) What is this? Some stay-bite to put you on until dinner time?

Zuleika No. It is the Princess's supper.

Jane The Princess's supper? (*She inspects the tray*) So little?

Zuleika The Princess is a dainty eater. Belike she will not eat all that I have prepared.

Jane Let me see. There is ...

Zuleika A leg and some few pieces of capon, a venison pasty, a morsel of cheese, a manchet of bread, a piece of marchpane and an apple.

Jane Marchpane—I am told that she is fond of sweetmeats. And to drink? What has she to drink?

Zuleika I have set both old ale and red wine. It is for her to choose.

Jane And she will sit here and eat as you or I would?

Zuleika This evening she will. She wished to be private. But first each item of food must be tasted by one of her ladies.

Jane Ah, the tasting! There are those who taste for the Queen. At Court, it is something of a ceremony.

Zuleika Here we do not stand on ceremony but I do not think that the Princess would wish to find you here at this time.

Jane You wish me to make myself scarce?

Zuleika nods

I am sped. (*She moves* R) I am departed. I am gone.

Jane goes out R

Zuleika is at first uncertain that she has indeed gone, and peers suspiciously after her. She goes over and looks off R. *After a careful survey, she seems reassured and returns for a final inspection of the tray*

Satisfied, Zuleika goes off L. *The chamber is empty for a moment or two, then Jane reappears* R, *walking on tiptoe. She approaches the tray circumspectly*

Jane The Princess's supper. No great repast, but I am sure it is well enough. (*She sits upon the stool intended as a seat*) It would be something to tell hereafter that one had eaten from the same dish as the Princess. (*She reaches out as if to take the capon leg but quickly draws back her hand*) No, no! She would have me whipped! (*A thought strikes her*) Why should I not taste the food and so save the ladies their labour? It would be a kindness to them. First, I will, as it were, sip this ale.

(*She takes up the pot, swigs heartily and smiles in appreciation*) Why, this is even better than Harvest ale! (*She swigs again*) But that is as it should be for this is company for royal fare. Now this capon—(*she picks up the capon leg, takes a bite and considers*)—is tender, tasty and all that might be expected of a bird in this situation. (*She continues to eat the capon leg*) Yes, this bird is of such quality that I can only regret that my acquaintance begins and ends with the leg. (*She sees the goblet*) Oh, the wine. I should sample the wine. (*She does so—generously*) Now this is none of your vile Rhenish but a lip-smacking French wine of sound body. (*She drinks again and tosses away the capon bone*) Yes, given enough of it, I could grow fond of such a wine. (*She picks up the pasty*) A venison pasty. It were best to see that it is fitting . . . (*She eats heartily*) And it is—there is even a touch of royalty in the seasoning. (*She munches away and, having set down the goblet, she picks up the tankard and, from time to time, imbibes great draughts of ale. Very soon, the tankard is empty and, to demonstrate the fact, she holds it upside down. When she speaks, her speech is slurred*) Now there is a strange thing—a very strange thing. I had but meant to taste the ale and now . . . (*The inverted tankard and her expression provide eloquent comment on the situation. She restores the tankard to the tray*) A morsel of cheese and a manchet of bread . . . (*She breaks off a piece and samples it*) Such bread! (*She expresses ecstasy*) I have never in my life tasted such—there's honesty in the crust, there's sustenance in it and oh!—it melts in the mouth. (*She savours it*) Some wine to wash it down. (*She takes up the goblet and drinks*)

Margaret comes in L, *sees Jane drinking and, horrified, halts in her tracks*

Margaret What is this? I am come to taste the Princess's food. It seems you have spared me the trouble.

Jane peers at her through narrowed eyes. She seems to be having difficulty in focusing and, when she speaks, appears bemused

Jane (*nodding*) That is so . . . Tasting . . . Saved you the trouble . . .

Margaret (*surveying the plundered tray*) What will she say? What will the Princess do? (*She runs off* L, *calling*) Emma! Nell! Rose! Quickly! Quickly! Jane has eaten the Princess's supper!

Margaret exits. In a moment all four enter L. *They surround Jane and contemplate the havoc before them*

Emma Some one of us should have been by to prevent this. We shall be blamed.

Nell (*glancing off* L) God help her! Here comes the Princess!

Emma and Nell help Jane to achieve an uncertain perpendicular

Elizabeth enters L

All four Ladies curtsy deeply. In seeking to achieve her own peculiar obeisance

—between a blundering bow and an awkward curtsy—Jane falls. Elizabeth remains immobile and stony-faced

Elizabeth One of you assist her.

But it needs both Nell and Margaret to get Jane back on her feet

What is here amiss?

Margaret (*apprehensively*) It is that Jane the Fool, your royal Highness, meaning no harm, I do believe, set herself to be taster of your food.

Jane (*more apprehensively still*) I was something over-zealous . . .

Elizabeth sweeps to inspect the tray and turns to Jane

Elizabeth You were indeed something over-zealous. (*She laughs at the expressions on the faces of those around her*) Over-zealous!

Emma Is she to be whipped, Princess?

Elizabeth Why, no! Here's no great matter.

Jane looks considerably relieved

I had no appetite for supper and I warrant she enjoyed the fare better than I would have done. (*She is suddenly stern*) There's this, Jane . . .

Jane Yes, your Grace?

Elizabeth You have had the supper. Now you must sing for it. (*She turns to her Ladies*) Must she not?

The Ladies make sounds of agreement. Jane moves, somewhat uncertainly, towards the centre of the chamber. Margaret moves the uncluttered stool to a position of advantage and Elizabeth sits upon it

Jane Sing . . . Yes, I will gladly sing if, by so doing, I may make amends. Now what shall it be? (*She considers and then smiles*) Some love song, belike?

Elizabeth (*shaking her head*) Not a love song. What say you, ladies?

All (*shaking their heads*) Not a love song.

Jane Then how say you to the tragical-comical song about the pedlar who arrives late at the inn. (*Brightly, she smiles round at them*)

Elizabeth (*shaking her head*) I think not, Jane. I am not in a tragical-comical mood. Not the pedlar. What say you, ladies?

All (*shaking their heads*) Not the pedlar.

Jane (*somewhat cast down*) Then I know not what will please you. (*Then, with sudden inspiration*) What of a drinking song?

Elizabeth (*judicially*) Now that I truly believe I would enjoy above all else. But I would not wish to impose my taste on the company. What say you to a drinking song, ladies?

The Ladies look enquiringly at one another and finally nod

Emma Above all things, we would like to hear a drinking song.

Elizabeth (*with a glance at the tray*) A drinking song will be most apt to the occasion.

All laugh except Jane, who looks sheepish

Jane This is an old song which, they say, goes back to King Stephen's day.

Margaret Perhaps, when we have heard it, we shall wish it had stayed there.

The Ladies laugh but Elizabeth raises a hand

Elizabeth Peace. Let her begin. Come, Jane.

Jane clears her throat and launches raucously into her song

Jane Back and side go bare, go bare,
   Both foot and hand go cold,
   But belly, God send thee good ale
   No matter new or old.
   I cannot eat but little meat,
   My stomach is not good
   But I do think that I can drink
   With him that wears a hood.
   Though I go bare, take you no care,
   I nothing am a-cold,
   I stuff my skin so full within
   With jolly good ale and old.
   Not frost, nor snow, nor wind I trow,
   Can hurt me if it wold,
   I am so wrapped within and lapped
   With jolly good ale and old.
   With jolly good ale and old.

There is applause from the small audience, which Jane acknowledges with an awkward bow

   (*Apologetically*) It is, your royal Highness, something of a short song.
Elizabeth That is but one of its merits. (*With a side glance at the tray*) I appreciated, in particular, the line, "I cannot eat but little meat".

The Ladies laugh

Jane You make mock of me but I take it in good part for you have laughed, mistress, for the first time since my coming hither.
Elizabeth She is in the right of it. As reward, Jane, you shall eat of my supper at some other time—and with my permission.
Jane I give thanks to your royal Highness. Would you now permit me to withdraw?
Elizabeth With my thanks, Jane. With my thanks.
Jane Before I leave you, good madam, may I entreat that, if I am again to eat of your supper, you ask them, on that occasion, to serve more generously of the capon—and of the ale.

Jane performs her peculiar obeisance and goes out R

Elizabeth laughs and signs to Margaret to follow Jane

Elizabeth Go after her. She could well fall upon the stair.

Margaret follows Jane off R

Emma (*who has been watching Jane's departure*) There is no harm in Jane—except an over-fondness for ale—and gluttony.

Elizabeth The patch is kind enough, but a huge feeder. (*She sighs and looks depressed*) And what shall we do now? How shall we fleet the time between now and bed-time?

Emma We could play chess.

Elizabeth (*petulantly*) That would be but two of us.

Emma We could have two boards in play and one could look on.

Elizabeth I am heart-sick of chess.

Nell (*brightly*) The lute-player is below stairs. I saw him but now. We could dance a galliard or two.

Elizabeth I am not for one galliard let alone two.

Rose Then I know your royal Highness to be truly out of spirits. I have never before known you refuse to dance a galliard.

Elizabeth There comes a first time for everything. I am weary—weary—weary of my life. What am I to do with what is left of my time?

Emma (*reproachfully*) Your royal Highness, it is better here than in the Tower.

There is a brief silence during which, it seems, Elizabeth considers the observation

Elizabeth It *is* better—but not greatly better.

Margaret returns. She curtsies and appears to be charged with suppressed excitement

Margaret Lady Alicia Mordaunt is here.

Elizabeth So late?

Margaret She comes from the Palace and is to return directly. She begs an audience of you.

Elizabeth If she must return directly, waste no time. Admit her at once.

Margaret curtsies and goes out R

I will see her here alone. (*She indicates the tray*) Remove these traces of Jane's repast.

Nell takes the tray and goes out L

Emma comes over to Elizabeth

Emma Your royal Highness has scarce eaten this day. When Lady Alicia has gone, will it please you to take a little supper?

Elizabeth No. I have no stomach for it.

Emma expresses disappointment

But, for your sake, I will take a cup of wine before I seek my bed. (*With a sudden flash of impatience*) But presently—presently . . . (*She waves them away*)

Somewhat puzzled by their abrupt dismissal, Emma and Rose curtsy and exit L

Elizabeth rises and paces restlessly to and fro

Why is she here so late? Why? (*She halts as Margaret enters*)

Margaret escorts Alicia into the chamber. Both Ladies curtsy to the Princess and Elizabeth makes a gesture of dismissal to Margaret, who goes out R

What brings you here so late, Lady Alicia?

Alicia I am come to take Jane the Fool back to the Palace. The Lord Chamberlain believes that the Queen should have all the people of her household about her at this time.

Elizabeth Now here is Palace ceremonial gone mad! Surely a royal heir may be delivered, acknowledged and proclaimed without the necessary attendance of the Queen's Fool!

Alicia You are, it seems, something behindhand with the news, your royal Highness. There is no question of a royal heir.

Elizabeth Has the Queen miscarried?

Alicia There never was the prospect of a child. The Queen, poor lady, deceived herself. She is mortally sick and is soon to die.

Elizabeth To die? The Queen is dying?

Alicia She was failing fast at the time of my leaving the Palace though it is thought she will yet linger some day or two. Her will has been made this long time past and your royal Highness is named as the undoubted heir.

Elizabeth Should I not go to her?

Alicia It would be to no avail. She would not be aware of your royal Highness's presence. There is but one person she would have wished to be with her at this time and he has been absent this long time past. It may be that now he has been crowned Emperor . . .

Elizabeth But they have sent to him?

Alicia They have sent, your royal Highness. But she will be dead before the couriers reach him.

Elizabeth turns away, moves a thoughtful pace or two and deliberates briefly. Then she turns again to Alicia

Elizabeth It still seems to me that I should go to her.

Alicia By no means, your royal Highness. You must not absent yourself from this place which is become the lodestone of all England. All over this realm are horses saddled in readiness and men stand booted and spurred.

Elizabeth To what purpose?

Alicia Why, they await the tolling of the Queen's passing bell. At the first knell, they will speed to pay homage to you, to assure you of their fealty, to swear allegiance to you and hope for some office of profit under the Crown. They will look for some signal mark of favour from yourself who are so soon to become the fount of honour for this nation.

Elizabeth (*awed*) Say you so—say you so . . .

Alicia I do assure you, Princess, that it will be so. I mean no disrespect to the poor Queen who lies so near to her last extremity for she has all but done with earthly ceremony. I would ask you: may I, as bringer of this news, be the first to kiss the hand of my sovereign lady that is soon to be?

Elizabeth (*uncertainly*) This, surely, is not something that I may well perform . . .

But Alicia is already kneeling at her feet. Almost hesitantly, Elizabeth extends her hand and Alicia kisses it. Then she looks up and regards Elizabeth steadily

Alicia I promise to be your liege of life and limb from this day forth until the hour of my death.

Elizabeth My thanks and blessing.

She helps Alicia to rise

And now, if you would send in my ladies . . .

Alicia (*curtsying*) Your royal Highness.

Elizabeth raises a detaining hand

Elizabeth A moment longer. You were kind to me, Lady Alicia, when the world was not. You will not need to spur to me if . . . When the bell shall toll. A place will be found for you.

Alicia (*curtsying*) I thank your royal Highness.

Alicia goes out R

Elizabeth sits on the stool

Elizabeth So prophecy is fulfilled and it would appear that Zuleika saw truly. I am delivered out of bondage and I have but to wait this little space for all my hopes and dreams to be realized. (*She reflects and sighs*) May my reign be longer and happier than poor Mary's. (*She rises from the stool and kneels*) O God, I thank Thee that Thou has sustained me through these years of travail until this present hour and I pray that Thou wilt grant me strength, courage and wisdom so that I may rule these people as they deserve. Amen. (*She is still kneeling when the Ladies come in but she rises almost at once*)

The four Ladies enter R. *Emma is carrying a goblet, and all four seem remarkably subdued. The other three stand off and regard Elizabeth as if she was now changed to them. Emma, however, approaches with the goblet*

Emma Lady Alicia has told us the news of the Queen, your royal Highness.

Elizabeth Then there is no need for me to repeat it.

Emma (*proffering the goblet*) The wine you asked for, your royal Highness.

Elizabeth (*taking it*) I thank you.

Margaret Your royal Highness, how shall we—know?

Elizabeth Know? (*She drinks some of the wine*)

Margaret About the Queen. If she . . .When she . . .

Elizabeth When she dies. Do not be afraid to speak of death—it is something we must all experience—once. Here, take this. I am not for wine.

She thrusts the goblet at Emma who takes it from her

How shall we know? (*She considers*) The bells of the city churches will toll a knell and this will be taken up by other churches throughout the land. Messengers, couriers, will ride day and night from London spreading the news that the Queen is dead. There will be—due ceremonies and I—I shall be proclaimed.

She is standing erect, shining-eyed and dazzled as she gazes into the near future. Emma signs to the others and they all kneel

Emma Your royal Highness——

Elizabeth turns and is surprised to see her ladies kneeling

—here be your four poor maids . . .

Rose Who have borne with you imprisonment, banishment and the threat of death.

Margaret We ask pardon if we have, at any time, failed you.

Nell If we did so, it was for want of sense and not for lack of goodwill.

Emma And we ask your blessing at this time.

Elizabeth (*smiling and extending her hands towards them in blessing*) Which is freely given. I bless you for you are my best and dearest and I thank you, thank you, for kindnesses without number and devotion without limit. Rise up. No princess was ever better served.

The Ladies rise and throng around Elizabeth to kiss her hands. Elizabeth smiles and reacts to the small flutter of excitement. Then her expression changes and the four Ladies move away and stand off regarding the Princess who appears distressed

Margaret What ails your royal Highness?

Elizabeth I would she were here.

Emma Who, your royal Highness?

Elizabeth Why, Kate Ashley. Kate Ashley, who has shared my troubles longer than any of you. Kate Ashley who was banished and was never dearer to me than at this moment. She should be here to share our joy and our deliverance.

Emma Never fear. She will hear the news.

Nell And she will come to you though the journey were a thousand miles.

Elizabeth (*smiling again*) So she will. So she will. I shall watch for her coming. (*She reflects briefly and then goes on in a different tone*) This may be the last night of waiting. For once, I could wish us to be more closely guarded. There are those who wish ill to our cause and it would be a tragic irony if I were to be struck down in this last hour.

Margaret We shall guard you.

Rose We shall defend you.

Emma With our lives if need be.

Elizabeth Then I shall sleep the sounder for knowing that you are on watch. (*She smiles on them*) Rest may be hard to come by tomorrow. You are to wake me if there comes any word from the Council. Give you good night and quiet guard.

Emma Good night and sweet repose to your royal Highness.

All four Ladies curtsy

Elizabeth acknowledges their curtsies with a grave nod, and goes out R

Margaret stands looking after her speculatively

Margaret Will she remember us hereafter, do you think . . . when she is Queen?

Emma You may be sure that she will. Those were not empty words that she spoke just now. (*She kindles at a thought*) Let us sing her to sleep with that chant we made for her. (*She flourishes the goblet*) I will rid me of this and see if that lute player is still to be found.

Emma is about to go when Rose checks her

Rose Remember that, at this hour, he may not come within the Princess's apartments.

Emma Do not trouble yourself—he shall stay on the bend of the stairs.

Emma hurries out L

Rose (*gazing after her, doubtfully*) Are we in the right to sing at this time of night?

Margaret We may well disturb the Princess.

Nell Princess . . . We must learn to address her as "your Majesty". But we shall not disturb her. You know her custom. She will read some little time before retiring.

Rose (*nodding*) Belike her *Book of Hours*.

Margaret I do not think that sleep will come easily to her tonight.

Nell I would not sleep were I in her case.

Emma returns. She is brisk, excited

Emma The lute player is in place. Come, make ready.

The three girls form into line. Emma calls off

NOW!

Emma then runs to take her place with the others and the lute (? guitar) player sounds a warning chord. Thereafter he plays accompaniment as the quartette sing a song which is something between a lullaby and an anthem

All Though much oppressed,
    And sore distressed,
    Take now your rest!
    Take now your rest!
    For you are blesséd!
    For you are blesséd!
    In peace abide!
    Cast care aside!
    All trouble shed
    As you lie abed.
    Thy strength is spent—
    It's time you went
    To healing sleep,
    Slumber profound,
    Let sense be drowned
    In slumber sound.
    Try counting sheep!

Here they raise their hands and, in unison, count sheep invisible to us

    Try counting sheep!

Counting is too much for Nell and she crumples, falls slowly, and is asleep

    Try counting sheep!
    Try counting sheep!
    Try counting sheep!

In the course of the repetition, Margaret and Rose slowly subside into slumber. Only Emma maintains a drowsy perpendicular and she is left alone to complete the song

Emma So quiet keep
    In your deep, deep,
    Sm—oo—thing,
    So—oo—thing
    Sl—ee—ee—p.

And, with this last word, she, too, succumbs. (She subsides on to one of the stools) A last, despairing discord suggests that the lute player has also fallen asleep. For a moment or two there is only the sound of snoring

  Elizabeth enters R. *She stands surveying her sleeping Ladies and enquires, between amusement and exasperation*

Elizabeth Who needs to fear when guarded by such vigilant sentinels? (*She shakes her head, claps her hands and calls out*) Rouse up, wantons! Awake! Awake! Rouse up! Come, bestir! Bestir! Awake! Awake!

Elizabeth's outcry wakes Emma, Nell and Margaret, who are troubled and shamed when they wake to see Elizabeth standing over them. They rise and, with some difficulty, get a very drowsy Rose on her feet—but still supported by her friends. Angrily, Elizabeth shouts

  Get you to bed!

It seems that the more wakeful trio will attempt a defence but Elizabeth points off R and commands

Go! As guards, you are useless!

Dragging the still unconscious Rose, the Ladies go off R

Elizabeth watches their departure, and repeats:

"Try counting sheep!"

Shaking her head, Elizabeth follows the Ladies off

The Light dies slowly in the chamber until total darkness prevails. (In the Black-out the stools are returned to their former places) A knell tolls its mournful message. The sound of the passing bell diminishes as a faint glimmer of light picks out the four Ladies standing once more in line, but now all are wearing the same dedicated, devoted expression. As they speak, the Light grows from a glimmer to a blaze

All Out of darkness, despair and death,
God sends our Elizabeth.
Out of darkness, death and despair,
Comes Elizabeth, undoubted heir,
Out of darkness, shedding light
Comes an angel, shining bright.

The Ladies take their places standing in line above the entrance R. When they have done so, there is a flourish of trumpets. As the flourish ends, a triumphant peal of church bells is heard near at hand

Elizabeth, more royal than we have ever seen her, enters R

She moves down to the centre of the chamber with her Ladies, two and two, some little way behind her, so that they do but provide a background to the blaze of royalty that is Elizabeth. The progress is checked and Elizabeth, smiling happily, looks off L. Then she throws wide her arms

Kate Ashley enters L and comes hurrying forward

Elizabeth and Kate embrace, and the sound of church bells dies away

Elizabeth Kate! Kate! My good Kate! You are here! Now is my joy in this day complete!

Elizabeth holds Kate at arms' length and regards her affectionately. It seems that she is about to enfold Kate again but the latter makes a gesture and gently disengages herself

Kate My sovereign lady, there is an office I must perform and that directly. (*She kneels before Elizabeth*) Give me now your hand to kiss.

Elizabeth does so

I promise, your Majesty, to be your liege of life and limb from this day forth until the hour of my death.

Elizabeth May that day be far distant.

She helps Kate to her feet and kisses her on the cheek

Dear Kate, I have missed you sorely every hour of every day that you have been away from me. (*Pointing*) Now stand you there at my right hand and share with me all that may chance this day.

Kate (*taking her place*) As your Majesty commands.

Elizabeth (*smiling*) "Your Majesty . . ." It will take me a short day and a long one before I become accustomed to being thus addressed. (*She reflects and the smile fades*) But my heart misgives me. This realm has been cruelly torn and misgoverned. This people has been oppressed and persecuted. Warring factions still bitterly oppose each other. Who am I to say that I will unite the people of this land?

Kate Who are you? I will tell you. You are Great Harry's daughter and you ascend the Throne of England by right of descent. You are the bright hope of this nation. You are the star by which they hope to be led. The prayers of a whole nation are yours. Men who have never prayed in their lives before say today: "God be thanked for our Elizabeth."

Elizabeth I would it were so. For I would not rule save by the people's favour.

Kate Their favour! You have their love! The Commons of England love you and they are here fully represented. On the day of your Coronation, they shall be thus addressed: "Sirs, I here present to you Queen Elizabeth, the rightful inheritor of the Crown, wherefore all ye that come here this day to do your homage, service and bounden duty, are you willing to do the same?"

With some initial encouragement from the Ladies who, as befits their station, are the first to answer, the representatives of the Commons of England reply

The Commons Yea! Yea!

Alicia, Harriet, Jane the Fool and Zuleika enter

Kate Here is the rightful and undoubted inheritor of the Crown of England by the laws of God and man and is elected, chosen and required by all three estates to take upon her the said Crown and royal dignity. Commons of England, do you accept her as your rightful and undoubted Queen?

The Commons Yea! Yea! We do! We do!

Once more, Kate makes the quelling gesture and then steps back leaving Elizabeth to face the Commons of England alone

Elizabeth My Lords and Commons of England, I do thank you from my heart for your acceptance of me. I am this day a proud woman for I am Queen of the English—a people brave, patient, persistent, enduring in the face of adversity and merciful in victory. Greatly do I respect your qualities and your unconquerable spirit, your hatred of tyrants and your love of liberty. We shall overthrow the dominion of the Pope of Rome and cast off the yoke of Philip of Spain! We shall sail oceans uncharted and win great victories by land and sea! Oh, my people, we shall do such deeds that the world will marvel at them and history will record them in such terms that men will say: "This was the great time! This was the great time of England!" Oh, I promise you, we shall do such deeds! Such deeds, my people!

Overcome, she bows her head and those on stage cry out

All God save the Queen! God save the Queen! God save Queen Elizabeth!

It is hoped that the Commons of England will here take up the cry and, at the proper moment, Kate will quell them with a gesture. Then those on stage will, anachronism or no, break into the first verse of the National Anthem. It is hoped—nay, expected!—that the Commons of England will join in

God save our gracious Queen!
Long live our noble Queen!
God save the Queen!
Send her victorious,
Happy and glorious,
Long to reign over us,
God save the Queen!

With Queen Elizabeth leading, followed by Kate, her Ladies, Lady Alicia, Lady Harriet and the rest, the Cast pass in procession through the audience which has, throughout, served as the faithful Commons of England. As the procession begins to move, the church bells begin their joyous pealing once again and—

the PLAY *ends*

FURNITURE AND PROPERTY LIST

ACT I

On stage: Throne set on dais. *Over it:* canopy with device of golden crown
2 stools

Off stage: Prayer book (Lady Jane Grey)
Belled bauble (Jane the Fool)

ACT II

Set: Stools in original positions

Off stage: Goblet (Harriet)
Tray with dishes and bowls containing pieces of capon, venison pasty,
cheese, bread, marchpane, apple; goblet of wine, tankard of beer
Goblet (Emma)

LIGHTING PLOT

The following plot gives cues that are essential to the action: further lighting changes can, of course, be inserted as facilities allow, at the discretion of the producer

Property fittings required: nil

An open stage. The same scene throughout

ACT I

To open: General overall lighting

Cue 1 **Lady Jane Grey** lays her head on stool and extends her
      arms   (Page 4)
      Black-out

Cue 2 After axe strikes block   (Page 4)
      Pause, then slow return to full lighting

Cue 3 **Elizabeth:** "This I say to you . . ."   (Page 24)
      Slow fade of general lighting to bright spot on Elizabeth

ACT II

To open: As Act I

Cue 4 **All:** "And pray, God, send it soon."   (Page 35)
      Black-out. Pause, then revert to previous lighting

Cue 5 **Elizabeth** follows **Ladies** off   (Page 46)
      *Slow fade to Black-out. As bell ceases to toll, revert to full
      lighting*

EFFECTS PLOT

ACT I

Cue 1 As CURTAIN rises   (Page 1)
        Fanfare of trumpets

Cue 2 **Margaret:** "One was for music."   (Page 1)
        Music: "Greensleeves"

Cue 3 **All:** ". . . Mary, who shall reign."   (Page 2)
        Flourish of trumpets

Cue 4 After Black-out when **Lady Jane Grey** places her head on
                stool   (Page 4)
        Sound of headsman's axe on block

Cue 5 **Margaret** and **Rose** exit   (Page 23)
        *Atmospheric music—dread and menace. Continue until
                dialogue resumes*

ACT II

Cue 6 **Mary, Alicia** and **Harriet** start to exit   (Page 33)
        Peal of bells—continue until exit

Cue 7 Lights fade to Black-out   (Page 46)
        Sound of passing bell

Cue 8 **Ladies** stand in line   (Page 46)
        *Flourish of trumpets followed by peal of bells—continue
                until **Elizabeth** and **Kate** embrace*

Cue 9 As Procession starts to move through audience   (Page 48)
        Peal of church bells

JANE'S SONG to the tune of *The Lincolnshire Poacher* (traditional)

(1) Back and si - de go bare, go bare, Both foot and hand go
(2) Though I go bare, take you no care, I no - thing am a —

cold —, But be - lly God send thee good ale No
cold —, I stuff my skin so full with in With

ma — tter new - or old — I can not eat but
jolly good ale and old — Nor frost, nor snow, nor

li - ttle meat, My sto - mach is — not good But —
wind I trow, Can hurt me if — it wold, I —

I do think that I can drink With him that wears a hood —.
am so wrapped with - in and lapped With jolly good ale and old —.

THE LULLABY with accompaniment of lute or guitar

Chords : I Iᵇ Vᶜ I I II II⁷ V

Andante Con Moto

Though much o - ppressed, And so - re di - stressed,

I Vᵇ V I VII⁷ V

Take now your rest! Take now your rest!

I V I IV I+ IV I—

For you are bless - ed! For you are bless - ed! In

II II⁷ V IVᵇ IV V I

pe - ace a - bide! Cast care a - side

I Iᵇ Vᶜ I Iᶜ Iᵉ II II⁷ V

All trou - ble shed As you lie — a - bed.

I Vᵇ V I II V V

Thy strength is spent — It's time — you went

IVᵇ V V I IV IV I

To hea - ling sleep, Slum - ber pro - found,

I I V I V

Let sense be drowned In slum - ber sound.

IV V I V I V I

Try coun - ting sheep! -ting sheep! -ting sheep!

I I I Iᵇ Vᶜ I

Sheep! Sheep! So qui - et keep

IV IV I I I

In your deep, smoothing, soothing, Slee -eep